T0356272

CHIEF RONDO

CHIEF RONDO

Securing Justice for the Murder of George Floyd

MEDARIA ARRADONDO
Former Minneapolis Police Chief

with Jennifer Amie

DIVERSION
BOOKS

Diversion Books
A division of Diversion Publishing Corp.
www.diversionbooks.com
Copyright © 2025 by Medaria Arradondo

Disclaimer: The names of certain individuals in this book have been changed to protect their privacy.

For more information, email info@diversionbooks.com

Hardcover ISBN: 978-1-63576-947-0
e-ISBN: 978-1-63576-943-2

Cover design by Jonathan Sainsbury
Design by Neuwirth & Associates, Inc.
Medaria "Rondo" Arradondo author photograph by Grace Stillman
Jennifer Amie author photograph by Jo Amie

Printed in the United States of America
10 9 8 7 6 5 4 3 2 1

Diversion books are available at special discounts for bulk purchases in the US by corporations, institutions, and other organizations. For more information, please contact admin@diversionbooks.com.

The publisher does not have any control over and does not assume any responsibility for author or third-party websites or their content.

To the children

May you never be left without hope on your journey

Let hope overcome fear and uncertainty,
and you will rise to become our better angels

You are the reason we strive for a brighter tomorrow

Contents

CHIEF RONDO

1

Black-Eyed Susans
Still Bloom

AT THE MINNEAPOLIS INTERSECTION OF THIRTY-EIGHTH STREET AND CHICAGO Avenue, a twelve-foot sculpture of a raised fist emerges from a bed of flowers. The memorial commemorates George Floyd, who was murdered on this corner on May 25, 2020. Former Minneapolis police officer Derek Chauvin pinned Floyd's back and neck beneath his knee until Floyd gasped his last breath, calling out for his mother as he died. Officers J. Alexander Kueng, Thomas Lane, and Tou Thao looked on with indifference. The tragedy was followed by the State and Federal criminal convictions of all four officers. The tragedy and the bittersweet triumph—one of America's greatest police-accountability victories—occurred on my watch.

In the spring and summer of 2020, I was three years into my term as the first Black chief of police in the history of the Minneapolis Police Department. I couldn't bring George Floyd back. But I could work on behalf of his family to bring them justice. That was my mission.

In the weeks after George Floyd's death, the city erupted with the most destructive and costly civil unrest in the United States since the LA riots twenty-eight years before. Decades of trauma, outrage, and frustration fueled the flames in cities across the country. For a time that summer, the whole world turned its focus on the legacy of American racial violence.

Today, visitors from around the world stand before the raised fist of resistance at Thirty-Eighth and Chicago. There, each summer, in late July, black-eyed Susans bloom, brightening the base of the sculpture with bursts of yellow petals. Grown from seeds harvested just a few blocks away, these flowers keep another memory alive. These black-eyed Susans are the direct descendants of blooms first planted in the 1930s by Mrs. Edith Lee.

For a time, Edith and her husband, Arthur Lee, owned a modest two-bedroom house at the corner of Forty-Sixth Street and Columbus Avenue. Arthur was a World War I veteran. He worked for the US Postal Service—a steady job with good pay, especially during the Great Depression. Their financial stability enabled the Lees to purchase a home in 1931. The little white house measured 850 square feet—a homey cottage where the Lees could raise their six-year-old daughter, Mary. The only problem with the house was the address. 4600 Columbus Avenue was located just south of a line that was invisible on the street map but existed nonetheless: a color line. Members of the local neighborhood association had voluntarily signed an agreement in 1927 to sell homes only to whites. Arthur, Edith, and Mary Lee were Black.

Neighbors posted a sign in the Lees' front yard soon after they moved in. It read: "No n—s allowed in the neighborhood. This means you." To regain white ownership of the house, the neighborhood association offered to buy it for $300 more than the Lees had paid. The family refused.

"Nobody asked me to move out when I was in France fighting in mud and water for this country," Arthur Lee told the *Minneapolis Tribune*. "I came out here to make this my home. I have a right to establish a home."

The Lees were members of the Minneapolis NAACP, which provided support by hiring Lena Olive Smith—the city's first, and only, Black female attorney. Smith met with the mayor and Police Chief William Meehan to discuss the tension brewing in the city. "As far as Mr. Lee is concerned," Smith told the *Tribune,* "there will be no further negotiations with any committee of citizens." At Smith's urging, Chief Meehan agreed to provide police protection for the Lee family and their home.

When neighbors learned that the Lees could not be bought out, they turned up the pressure. Vandals threw black paint on the little white house. The Lees received death threats. Mary's dog died of poisoning. On July 11, 1931, about 150 people stood outside the Lees' home to protest and intimidate the family. Five days later, the Lees' house was surrounded by more than 3,000 angry whites and onlookers. The *Tribune* described the scene on July 16:

> From the windows of his darkened home, Lee and his friends looked out, as from a barricaded fortress, on a sullen, angry semicircle of humanity. They heard themselves threatened continually, from all directions. They heard stones strike against the house and heard windows crash as some of the stones took effect. Now and then a firecracker exploded on the lawn.

World War I service veterans from Arthur Lee's American Legion post, along with members of the postal workers' union, arrived to defend the family around the clock. The Lees later told their grandson, Robert Arthur Lee Forman, that these supporters had joined hands to form a human barricade between the family and the crowd. They were hoping to prevent "what truly could have been a horrific tragedy," said Forman.

Chief Meehan initially deployed a squad of twenty-five officers to guard the home. At first, the officers were able to break up the crowd, but they were soon vastly outnumbered. An NAACP observer documented the violence and vitriol the mob directed at the Lees:

> Yells of "let's rush the door," "let's settle this now," "let's drag the n—s out"; the clatter of glass being knocked from the windows by stones; the flash of photographers' torches, and the bursting of firecrackers, created a revel of morons.

The crowd included men, women, and children. Vending wagons arrived to sell ice cream and refreshments. From evening until the early hours of the morning, shouts and slurs and other harassments rained down on the little white house, forcing the Lee family to sleep in the basement. The crowd was defiant of the police, the *Tribune* reported.

> Standing ten feet apart, [the police officers] waited. Inch by inch the crowd moved closer to the Lee home, muttering threats, and loud in their denunciation of the police. More police reserves were sent for. A squad of motorcycle men mounted their machines. They drove straight at the crowd, turning sharply as they reached the front lines. This only served to rouse the throng. One motorcycle policeman was pulled from his machine and a squad of patrolmen went charging to his rescue.

Every available squad rushed to the scene. The crowd was undeterred, advancing toward the Lee home until the throng stood almost face-to-face with the line of policemen. Day after day, the officers stood their ground against a barrage of taunts and threats and rocks.

The mob of thousands persisted until the newspapers published a definitive statement on July 20 from attorney Lena Olive Smith that the Lees were not going to leave their home. "Mr. Lee intends to remain in his present residence," it said. "He has no intention of moving now or later. . . . I believe we have made that clear to all parties involved. I have been assured that my client will receive ample police protection." The crowd began to shrink, but it took a month for the nightly protests to disband. For more than a year, the Lee family remained under police protection. Mary had to be escorted to and from kindergarten by a uniformed officer.

I often think of the conversations that Arthur and Edith Lee might have had as they peeked through their curtains at the furious mob. I wonder if they asked themselves whether taking a stand was worth it. Their lives had been threatened. Surely, they worried about putting their child in danger. At the same time, their hopes for Mary's future must have fueled their determination. The Lee family inhabited their home until late 1932, when they chose to move to a more integrated neighborhood nearby. They felt they had stayed long enough to make a point. They were not second-class citizens.

Just eleven years prior, three Black circus workers had been lynched by a white mob in Duluth, Minnesota. It would be another thirty-three years before the passage of the Civil Rights Act of 1964. But the Minneapolis police officers of 1931—most of them white— showed up night after night to stand between a riotous crowd of thousands and a Black family of three. Some of the officers might not have been able to afford a house like the Lees'. Some of the officers took a beating. I'm sure there were some who were asking: "Why am I putting myself in harm's way for this?" But they showed up anyway. They followed the orders of a police chief who had come to America at the age of twelve and whose own family may have faced discrimination as Irish immigrants in the 1880s.

The chief and officers of 1931 demonstrated what Chauvin, Kueng, Lane, and Thao failed to understand. Police officers are granted their power by the citizens they serve—and with that power comes the obligation to protect the rights and safety of all people. It's as true today as it was then. When someone calls 911 because they need help from the police, they reach a dispatcher—a total stranger. The dispatcher doesn't ask the caller anything about their social status in life—nothing about the caller's income, who they love, who they worship, or what party they vote for. It's just: Where are you? What's the emergency? We're on our way.

Meanwhile, the caller doesn't know anything about the police officer sent in response. This blind trust is rare today, but it is essential to the contract between citizens and the police. Policing is the only profession in which a member can detain a person, deprive them of their freedom, and legally take their life. Even the president doesn't have that authority. If there's ever a system that needs oversight and accountability, it's policing. Time and again, the system has failed to provide consequences for officers who kill, harm, or mistreat citizens. It leads to civil unrest.

The combination of peaceful protest and destructive turmoil following George Floyd's murder in 2020 was unprecedented in scale, but it was by no means the first uprising against the Minneapolis Police.

The people's quest for police accountability has spanned generations. During the long, hot summers of the 1960s, tension between Black community members and police in Minneapolis erupted in violence. Riots in 1966 and 1967 were a culmination of many forces in play during the civil rights era. The *Minneapolis Tribune* observed, "Negro youths in the cities of America also are expressing a profound sense of indignation for their group, a group striving to gain its rightful place in society not later, but now." The previous summer, after a riot in North Minneapolis, politicians had promised to invest in jobs for Black youth. That promise, however, went unfulfilled.

According to Minneapolis civil rights leader W. Harry Davis and other community members, the 1967 uprising was sparked when a white bar owner shot a Black man. Others said the tipping point occurred at the city's Aquatennial Torchlight Parade, an event that is still held every summer. Police officers intervened in a fight between two Black teenage girls by shoving the girls to the ground. All we have is the oral record. There was no video. But we know in the Black community, oral history contains essential knowledge. We pass down stories to survive and learn. Either of these incidents would have been enough to push young Black people over the edge.

Protesters marched on the night of July 20, 1967, the night after the Aquatennial Torchlight Parade. They demanded an end to violence against Black people—most of all by the police. Officers in riot gear responded, and one is reported to have struck a pregnant woman in the belly—further enraging the protesters. Some in the crowd threw rocks and bottles at police and broke store windows. Along an eight-block stretch of Plymouth Avenue North, protesters set stores and other businesses on fire.

W. Harry Davis and Urban League director Josie Johnson were summoned by the mayor to help bring peace to a neighborhood that was now losing its community resources. All three of the grocery stores on Plymouth Avenue burned that night. Davis described the destruction:

There was only fire—fire everywhere, it seemed—and scared, agitated people milling about. . . . The scene that night on the street was nightmarish. The stench of smoke was oppressive. The heat was enough to break display windows, exposing the stores to looting. The streets were blocked.

On July 21, Minneapolis mayor Arthur Naftalin appealed to the governor to deploy the Minnesota National Guard. The next day, six hundred troops arrived in North Minneapolis and the unrest was over. It had resulted in eighteen fires, thirty-six arrests, three shootings, and twenty-four injuries. Damages along Plymouth Avenue totaled $4.2 million—the equivalent of $32.5 million in 2020.

In the aftermath, Mayor Naftalin convened an all-white grand jury to investigate the cause of the riots. The move was widely regarded as an act by Naftalin to de-legitimize the concerns of Black residents. Unsurprisingly, this grand jury found no wrongdoing by police. Instead, they advised that the staff of the neighborhood's Black community center, The Way, should be investigated for inciting the unrest. These findings had no credibility within the Black community.

The *Minneapolis Tribune* offered an analysis of the unrest in the summer of 1967 that could apply just as easily to the summer of 2020: "The racial disturbances in a city such as Minneapolis are not just the result of unemployment, poor housing and discrimination, although these are likely factors. The disturbances also may be a part . . . of a broader malaise of youth."

I remember speaking to a group of young people in North Minneapolis in 2021 and hearing this malaise in the voice of a young man about twenty years old. He raised his hand and said to me, "Chief, I'm tired of slow justice." The only thing I could tell him was, "I understand." The generation that raised me was tired of slow justice before I was born. I have lived a long time myself, and I have not yet seen swift justice. But sometimes a big swing results from cumulative actions over time.

Mary Lee was six years old when she needed police protection just to walk to school. She was forty-three years old by the time the Fair Housing Act was passed, making racial discrimination in housing illegal. But after her family's courageous stand in 1931, there was never another mob in Minneapolis protesting outside the home of a Black family. We must continue to move forward. No matter how frustrated or how tired I get, I am never going to give up. Progress is not always linear, as we will see in the following chapters. Broken systems have a natural tendency to embrace stasis and to follow the path of least resistance. Nevertheless, individuals within institutions—and outside of them—can make a difference, for better or for worse.

I often thought of the children of the city during the tumultuous summer of 2020. You can imagine the concerns of children who may have seen a man's life extinguished on video. They have watched thousands of people marching in the streets and seen neighborhoods burning. A frightening pandemic has shut down their classrooms and disrupted the comfort of their regular routines. In times like this, children want to be reassured, and they look to adults for answers. They wonder if we are going to get through this—or if this is the way it's going to be from now on. As a leader and as a father, I didn't always have the answer. I certainly didn't have a playbook to guide me in 2020. But I was certain of one thing. There was no way I was going to leave the children of our city a legacy of despair.

There are four generations of Medaria Arradondos living in Minneapolis today. Most people call me Rondo, but my given name is Medaria, after my father and my grandfather. My son and grandson also bear this family name. The littlest Medaria Arradondo is still a preschooler and he will be brought up, like I was, to recognize the importance of hope. Unlike wishful thinking, hope acknowledges the challenges we face and says we can overcome them.

If American democracy is an experiment, as it has been described throughout our history, American policing is also an experiment that we are constantly trying to get right. We must call out the impediments that slow our progress and try to disrupt the forces that stand in the way of justice for all. We have seen police live up to their oath, honorably, and we have seen them fail. With the level of responsibility and authority that is granted to the police, when we fail the consequences are severe.

Even though we are making incremental progress, we cannot detach policing from its history. That history is always with us and cannot be revised or erased. Some look at our imperfect history as an anchor that weighs our profession down. In one sense, that's true. You can't run away from who you are. We must acknowledge our vulnerabilities and learn from our mistakes. And we should never forget how much police contribute to our communities when we are at our best. An anchor, like our history, can be a stabilizing force. I look to our past not as a burden but as a touchpoint that grounds me in turbulent times. Our history shows us how far we have come, how far we have yet to go, and what direction we need to move forward.

2

A Son of Minneapolis

IN THE SUMMER OF 1978, WHEN I WAS ELEVEN YEARS OLD, I SET OUT EACH MORNING at 6:00 a.m. to deliver the *Minneapolis Star Tribune* newspaper (rebranded in 2024 as the *Minnesota Star Tribune*). The job didn't pay much, but it helped contribute to the family budget and it kept me flush with Tootsie Rolls and Charms Blow Pops. When I arrived on my blue Huffy to pick up the morning edition from the distributor, I was the lone kid among all the adult carriers—and mine was the only bike among all their cars.

Pedaling through the dark streets, I towed a broken-down yellow wagon rigged up to the back of my bike. The wagon contained the papers and my eight-year-old brother, Johnny. I had placed a few blankets and a pillow in there so Johnny could be comfortable—but sometimes he had to sit on top of the papers. It had not been my idea to haul a sleepy second-grader along on my route. But when I had proudly told my mother about my new job, she said, "Take your brother with you." That's the way it was in a large family. You were always looking after someone, and you always had someone looking out for you.

I grew up with my parents and nine siblings in a large, white two-story house on the 3700 block of Park Avenue South in Minneapolis. A pile of kids' shoes in all sizes waited just inside the front door to trip any visitors who failed to watch their step. We ate meals on a variety of mismatched plates, accumulated in different patterns and colors. Apparently, the size of our family far exceeded the number of place settings in a standard set of dishes. Our pantry was crowded with canned goods to feed a lot of growing kids. My dear mother was a chef Houdini! She could do magic with a couple of cans of cream of mushroom soup.

Although our home was bustling with children, my mother always kept it clean. You know that saying "you can eat off the floor"? The Minnesota Department of Health would have applied it to my house. My mother's neatness extended to our clothes and appearance. We may not have been able to afford the highest quality clothes, but they were freshly laundered and neatly folded. The Arradondo kids were not walking out that front door with stains or wrinkles. These standards had nothing to do with social status—to this day, my parents don't measure anyone's worth by what they can buy. Rather, making an effort in your appearance was seen as self-respect and self-care. I've tried to live up to that credo, and I've tried to pass it on.

Unfortunately, I did not inherit all the traits I admire in my parents. Although I can't draw to save my life, my father is a talented artist, particularly as a painter. He will spend years adding the slightest, but powerful, details to his canvases. I remember one beautiful painting that had a bare tree in the background, which was not the central focus of the portrait. After several years he added leaves to it.

When I asked him why, after so many years, he added this detail, he simply said, "It was time."

Don't let my mother Jackie's petite stature fool you. She's a powerful presence and loves fiercely. She's strong and resilient, yet soft-spoken. When she speaks, you are drawn in to listen. My parents are living examples of how to treat others with respect, and they instilled a sense of service in their children. Growing up with nine siblings was a life lesson in and of itself. I had to advocate for myself and I had to compromise. With different ages, interests, and personalities, all of us kids were rarely in agreement—and so I came to understand that agreement is not a prerequisite for civility or friendship.

When I was a kid, the South Side was a neighborhood of working- and middle-class Black families, many of whom owned their homes. From the 1930s to the 1970s, there were more than twenty Black-owned businesses in the corridor along Thirty-Eighth Street and Fourth Avenue South. Among them was *Minneapolis Spokesman* (now the *Minnesota Spokesman-Recorder*), the oldest continuously operated Black newspaper in Minnesota, founded in 1934 by Cecil Newman. As kids, our neighborhood headquarters was Phelps Park, with its grassy lawns, picnic tables, ballfields, and playground. That's where I met up with my friends after school and during long summer days. If you had a crush on a girl and wrote her a letter, you handed it to her at the park. It was the site of weekend family cookouts, baseball games, and daring feats on the monkey bars. Second only to Phelps Park were the alleys that carved a kid-sized thoroughfare through the middle of each block. We ran up and down these corridors like we owned the place, stopping on hot days to take a drink from a neighbor's hose or spigot, always being careful to turn off the water when we were through. We'd spend hours building wooden ramps on stacks of bricks to do Evel Knievel jumps with our bikes. It's a wonder we survived the landings.

In those days, most homes in the neighborhood, like our house, did not have central air-conditioning. The smells of lasagna or chicken wafting out of open windows told you exactly what each family would be serving for dinner. This airborne preview gave me time to decide whether I should go home at six like I was supposed to or make an excuse to tag along with a friend who was having something really special. The choice was clear whenever my mother made pork chops—nothing could compare.

The neighborhood felt like an extended family to me. As kids, we knew all the adults on the block, and we only called them by their last names. They encouraged us to be our best selves. Any adult had the leeway to give you public praise if you were minding your manners or to discipline you if you were out of line. Children were viewed as priceless assets of the community, a source of pride and bright potential, regardless of whatever financial or familial struggles impacted their home life. The guiding lights in our community were—and still are today—the Black church and our elders. I have learned that nothing in the Black community moves forward in Minneapolis without the Black church behind it. Even when I had an office in City Hall, Zion Baptist Church on the North Side served as my satellite location.

When I was growing up, elders provided guidance and received our deep respect. One day, I watched an elderly Black woman walk down the street toward a group of older teenagers who were hanging out on the corner, smoking cigarettes. The teens were part of what you could call a gang at that time. The younger kids viewed them as the rough crowd, and I was amazed at the four-letter words I sometimes overheard them say. As soon as the elderly woman drew close to those young men, their cigarettes disappeared behind their backs. Every single one of them stood up straight—they looked to me like soldiers in a military parade. The teens nodded their heads and addressed the woman by name. "Good afternoon, Mrs. Jenkins, yep, have a good day." The cigarettes and smack talk only re-emerged when she was well down the block and out of earshot.

The teenagers' behavior was not merely a nostalgic display of old-fashioned manners. Nor was there the slightest hint of mockery in their tone or actions. The teens adhered to a social code that applied to everyone. There was a shared recognition in our community that while our elders were people we looked up to, they were also in the stage of life when we must look after them. These informal yet deeply ingrained customs and expectations helped keep the community safe.

Years later, as a patrol officer in North Minneapolis, I heard a call-in show on KMOJ, the local Black-owned radio station, that took me right back to that encounter on the corner. But in this case, the social code had broken down and needed repair. An elderly woman called in and said to the DJ, "I wonder if I might be able to get some help. I'm older and living on Social Security. I take the bus to wash my clothes at the laundromat on Broadway. The last couple of times, some young boys were standing around and blocking the door. I don't feel safe. I haven't been able to do my laundry in a couple of weeks."

I pulled my squad car over in a huff and debated driving down to Broadway myself. Then the DJ said, "Ma'am, please hold on. I'm going to talk to you off the air." On the air he said, with an undertone of indignation, "Men out there, meet me at the laundromat on Tuesday. We're going to make sure she's able to wash her clothes." I didn't drive to the laundromat myself, because it wasn't necessary. I had no doubt that, on Tuesday, the kids' behavior would be corrected by adults in the community.

Some of the elders I once knew have passed away. Many of my friends, now grown, have moved away. Still, when I visit family members who live in South Minneapolis, I often run into young adults who were just pipsqueaks, as we called them, in my youth. They are now raising their own families nearby.

The pipsqueak generation is too young to remember the long-gone landmarks of my childhood, such as Wilharm Pharmacy. It had a soda fountain in the back. Mr. Wilharm knew his customers and would give neighborhood families credit if you were coming up a bit short—simply on your word that you'd pay him back.

The pharmacy was long ago replaced by a convenience store. A crooked banner with the word "Unity" written on black vinyl now hangs above the awning out front. This banner only partially covers the large red letters that spell out "Cup Foods" across the brick storefront. This is the intersection of Thirty-Eighth and Chicago today—rich in unsung heritage yet struggling to move forward following the tragedy that occurred here: the murder of George Floyd in 2020. I've known this corner my whole life. That's long enough to understand that while much has changed, the resilience of the people is a constant. There was widespread destruction in the summer of 2020. But for every shattered window, there were dozens of neighbors who showed up with brooms to sweep away the shards.

In the 1970s, there were very few officers in the Minneapolis Police Department who looked like me. One was the late Riley Gilchrist, a tall, thin man who wore glasses and spoke in a deep baritone. In uniform he was a hybrid police/professor, an impression magnified when he was smoking a cigar. Officer Gilchrist cared about the community and coached Minneapolis Park Board youth football. When he came walking down the block, it was like Moses parting the Red Sea. As a kid I thought, "Wow! Here is a police officer who is serving the neighborhood and being respected for it."

Not only were there few Black police officers in my neighborhood growing up, I saw few police officers at all. At that time, a kind of self-reliance threaded through the fabric of our community. Today it is topical to talk about safety beyond policing—but alternatives to traditional 911 police response were practiced every day back then. Neighborhood disputes were resolved by elders and neighbors.

When police were called in, a different dynamic held sway. Other than Officer Gilchrist, most police officers were strangers. Their job was to resolve a situation quickly so they could move on to the next call. These officers did not always demonstrate the compassion or empathy that we were used to when resolving conflicts on our own—so we kept our guard up.

This ambivalence toward police first hit me when I was eight years old. One night, I was awakened by my father telling my mother to call the police. I walked out of my bedroom to the landing at the top of the stairway, where I could see across the living room into the kitchen. Standing there in my pajamas, I heard sounds coming from the basement—first the sound of kicking, then glass breaking. I heard a voice from below that seemed to be asking: "Where are you?" I saw my father placing a chair up against the door that led to the basement, jamming it shut.

After what seemed like an eternity but was probably only minutes, two white male police officers came into our house through the front door with their guns drawn. "Where is the intruder?" they asked, as my father directed them toward the basement door. While removing the chair from beneath the doorknob, my father recognized something in the voice coming from below. It was his cousin's voice.

Like millions of Americans, my father's cousin struggled with mental health issues and today would likely have been diagnosed with bipolar disorder. Back then, mental health services in the Black community were either nonexistent or woefully inadequate. The stigma associated with depression and trauma, especially for Black men during the 1970s, was heavy and hard. As a consequence, a mental health crisis was playing out in our basement.

The two police officers were right behind my father, guns raised and ready to descend the stairs. My father stood between them and the basement door.

My father is an eloquent speaker. His voice conveys confidence. But that night, as my father stepped aside to allow the officers down the basement stairs, I heard desperation in his plea: "Please don't shoot him! He's my cousin."

Watching silently from the landing, I wondered why my father was so concerned that the police might shoot a man who I thought would never try to harm us, even if he was struggling. Fortunately, nobody was hurt that night. But it was my first glimpse of the reality that adults—even my father—could be afraid. And that calling the police could possibly end in tragedy.

3
The Boot

AFTER GRADUATING FROM MINNEAPOLIS ROOSEVELT HIGH SCHOOL, I WENT ON TO
receive degrees in criminal justice from Suomi College in Hancock,
Michigan, and Metropolitan State University in St. Paul, Minnesota.
In 1989, I graduated from the police academy and became a recruit
officer with the Minneapolis Police Department. My parents were
proud that I was the first in our family to wear a police uniform, and
I was proud to represent my family in taking on this service.

I was just twenty-two years old, but I was not naive about the
profession. Being born and raised as an African American kid in
Minneapolis, I had elders who gave me lessons about the city and
about life. They imparted the historical knowledge often left out of
textbooks and newspapers but recorded in the memories of community members. I knew the history of policing in Minneapolis as
it related to the Black community. I had been schooled by the best,
and they helped shape my ideas about what kind of officer I wanted
to be.

Growing up as part of a community whose members have often been pre-judged by the police, I wanted to be an officer who showed up with an open mind. I knew that police officers make a difference during people's worst moments and can offer a sense of hope when it is needed most. We all hear stories of ordinary people doing extraordinary things to help others who they don't even know—a stranger jumping in a lake to save a drowning child, or passersby pulling a family from a burning house. I think most of us get a chill up our spine when we hear of such selflessness. Often, we ask ourselves: Could I have done that? When these brave individuals are interviewed on the news, with their singed eyebrows and smoke-stained clothes, they almost always say: "I had to do it. I wasn't going to stand by and let that person get hurt." I was about to meet and work alongside many courageous, selfless people who, like these Good Samaritans, were willing to put themselves in harm's way to help a stranger. Instead of simply being in the right place at the right time, these officers had signed on to go toward the danger every day. That's why we say this profession is a calling.

The night before my first day as a recruit, I pressed my uniform shirt, making sure the crease was sharp enough to slice a loaf of bread. I had a ritual for polishing my boots: cotton balls, cold water, and black shoe polish. I buffed them to a nice shine. I made sure my uniform was meticulous because my name tag said "M. Arradondo." That meant I needed to live up to both my inspector's standards and my mother's. "You represent us," my mother would say—and she had taught me that one's appearance matters.

In Minneapolis, the department gave you the hat and the badge, but you had to pay for your uniform pants and shirts and your equipment—a flashlight, a leather duty belt, and a gun. I had scraped together enough to buy everything but the gun. The pay for our rookie class was so low we were close to qualifying for food stamps, and I had no money left. So, I reached out for help. I made a call to W. Harry Davis. I had grown up with his son and spent many afternoons at the Davis house. I was always welcome and never left without receiving a history lesson from the renowned civil rights leader who, among many other accomplishments, had helped bring calm to Plymouth Avenue after the 1967 riots. Mr. Davis was a veteran of historic conflicts between the police department and the city's Black community. Yet it never entered my mind that he might object to helping me complete my uniform. That's not the kind of man he was. I only worried he might have sticker shock over the price. He did ask me, "How much is the gun?" When I told him, he replied, "I'm in a meeting right now, but you come on down." When I arrived, he had a check waiting for me. And when I entered my new profession, I brought with me the lessons learned from many years of observing Mr. Davis interact with people of all races to pursue a common cause: improving the lives of people in our city.

Everything I had trained for at the academy was starting now. I was about to enter the Field Training Officer program. As excited as I was, I knew better than to get too puffed up about it. I was about to become a "Boot." That was the term for all new recruits. It signified that we were nothing at this point.

At that time, the Minneapolis Police Department ran three shifts to cover twenty-four hours: day shift (6:00 a.m.–2:00 p.m.), mid-shift (2:00 p.m.–10:00 p.m.), and dogwatch (10:00 p.m.–6:00 a.m.). I've been told that "dogwatch" is a sailor's term for the hours when, on land, all but the dogs are asleep.

I started out on the mid-shift in the 4th Precinct, which covered downtown Minneapolis. Every patrol shift starts with roll call—the time when supervisors give their daily or nightly briefs, the equivalent of a parent providing the kids an overview of what their family vacation is about to look like before everybody piles into the station wagon. The supervisor stands at a podium, sharing information on new policies, changes in the law that officers need to know, and hot spots in the precinct. The supervisor might say: "Squad 411, be aware that they're expecting a large crowd at the downtown bar rush tonight. If you guys go up to the diner, make sure you're tipping the waitstaff good. They don't have to keep the place open all night but they do it to take care of us." Roll call is also a time for a sergeant to recognize personal and professional milestones: "Officer Swanson is getting married next week, so give him a hard time—it's the worst decision he ever made."

Roll call gives senior officers a chance to review any issues from the previous day. The veteran officers were informal coaches, pointing out what could have been done better. In those days, the senior officers sat and sipped their coffee or had a "spit cup" for their chewing tobacco. Many came from a generation where smoking cigarettes was as common as carrying a cell phone today. This was before indoor smoking bans, and some senior officers walked in with a "heater" dangling from their mouth, having mastered the ability to hold a conversation without ever dropping the lit cigarette.

If the chairs were full when a senior officer walked in, a Boot would give up his or her chair immediately and go stand in the back of the room. When I walked into roll call on my first day, I took my place alongside three other recruits standing at the back. After the daily brief, the sergeant threw out a question that prompted many senior officers to shrink down in their chairs, as if this would render them temporarily invisible.

"Who's going to take the Boots?" the sergeant asked.

If no one volunteered, the sergeant would issue assignments. A chosen officer might protest that he had just trained a Boot last month and now it was someone else's turn. A Boot was like the younger sibling that your mother forced you to take along on a date. No one was going to have a good time.

After some haggling, the first three Boots were paired with officers. My name was called last. "Okay, we've got recruit Arradondo," said the sergeant. A hush fell over the room. As the silence stretched on, I thought: "It's gonna be bad if everyone walks out of the room and I'm still standing here when the lights go off!" Finally, I heard a gruff voice speak up. "Yeah, I'll take the Arradondo kid."

The officer who selected me had more than twenty years on the force. I'll call him Officer Johnson, and he was known around the force for never going the full distance and always looking for a way to deliver the least amount of work during his shift. And so Officer Johnson was nicknamed "Short Cut." He was a white man in his early fifties, which was considered old back then. His slick black hair was streaked with gray. His leather gear was worn and his boots never shined. Rather than iron his shirt, he put on his uniform jacket to cover up the wrinkles. He spoke fast and seemed preoccupied with his own troubles. He always let somebody else drive so that he could work on his personal business while on the clock. In hindsight, I can confirm that Officer Johnson is the last person you'd ever want training anybody. I didn't know that at the time, and even if I had, it wouldn't have made a difference: The alternative was no training at all.

As roll call ended, Officer Johnson immediately began issuing instructions. There was no handshake, no introduction—just: Grab the shotgun and make sure you've got these supplies. As we walked out to his squad car he looked at me and said, "Let me tell you, kid, here's the only reason why I took you. You got an uncle named John?" I said, "Yep, that's my uncle." Officer Johnson continued, "When I was a kid, I got into a few scraps and I went to the county juvenile home. Your uncle took care of me when I was in there. That's the only reason I'm taking you."

With that preamble, I was not surprised by what he said next: "You're going to be driving every shift. I handle the radio—you don't touch it. You go where I tell you to go. You're going to be doing all the paperwork." This slight hazing was typical for Boots. From the training officer's point of view, a Boot had to prove worthy of being part of the team. Before we let you in, the thinking went, you've got to show us you can hold your own. When lives are on the line, it's crucial that every member of the team can perform reliably, not only on their best day, but also on their worst day.

Patrol officers are the ones rushing into gunfire when others are rushing away. They are called into people's lives when emotions are high and outcomes uncertain. On any given shift, they might find themselves searching for a lost child, calming a robbery victim, or pulling an injured driver from a burning car. When these are the stakes, the training manual alone isn't going to cover it. The way the patrol officers looked at it, recruits must also be evaluated through the lens of practical experience—and patrol experience is what counts. The inspector is at home sleeping. He works Monday through Friday! Only the patrol officers are out dealing with a rowdy Saturday night bar crowd at 2:00 a.m. The chief isn't riding around in a squad car. Patrol officers called City Hall the "chocolate factory," where everything for the higher-ups is rainbows and candy.

We, on the other hand, were in the sweatshop. A badge of honor for a squad was how many log sheets you filled out during a shift, describing the calls you went on. At thirty calls per sheet, you were humping if you ended the shift with a stack of log sheets. On a busy Saturday night you never wanted to be that squad that came in with half a log sheet. The day-to-day work of a patrol officer involves long days and nights. There are times when nobody even gives you a simple thank-you. The hours can be crappy, and you're not compensated as well as you should be. Despite all that, most officers show up to do a professional job that requires them to stand between the community and harm. They're not doing it for the accolades, but when the community does show appreciation, it is deeply felt.

Every Boot was expected to work every holiday, even if you had a family. My first several years, I ate many holiday meals in the precinct basement, where officers brought in potluck. At Thanksgiving and Christmas, however, every precinct in the city of Minneapolis had as many turkeys and hams as we could eat, all dropped off by members of the community. People knew that while they were home with their families on those bitter cold nights, we were working. Restaurants called up to say, "Have your officers stop by. If they can't stay, we'll have food ready to go for them." Strangers pulled up in the parking lot with pies. All communities contributed their comfort foods, from Southeast Asian to African to Mexican specialties and many more. I don't know of any precinct officer during the holiday season who doesn't put on weight. They're being fed by the kindness of people's hearts.

As a Boot, you don't know anything yet. At first, you're not allowed to do anything either. Just watch and learn. You literally don't count. Even though there are two humans in the squad car, dispatch only counts one because Boots are useless. Eventually, Boots can take on more tasks and are looked on as part of a two-person squad. In the final phase of training, the Boot does everything while the training officer evaluates their performance. At this stage, your survival in the department is in the hands of your training officer.

When I was a Boot, there were no formally designated, specially trained Field Training Officers. It was the luck of the draw for recruits, whose experience was more like an initiation than an education. Today's Field Training Officers must apply for the role, take classes, and pass exams. But I landed a trainer based on a chance connection to my uncle—so my instruction focused on Officer Johnson's principal policing interest. His claim to fame was ticket writing. He had a method for it. He drove downtown to Eighth Street between Hennepin Avenue and Third Avenue, where there are a number of high-rise office buildings. At 5:00 p.m. he was in position, staking out the no parking zone. As cars pulled up and double-parked so the drivers could pick up a friend or spouse from work, Officer Johnson would ticket them.

Now Officer Johnson was going to pass his technique along to me. He deposited me on the sidewalk along Eighth Street and said, "Okay, kid, you start up here and write out tickets for all these cars and I'll start at the other end of the street. We'll meet in the middle." He came prepared with a stack of ticket books already partially filled out.

I was sympathetic to the people just trying to get home from work. I didn't want to give the drivers tickets if I could simply move them along. So I would approach the driver and say: "Sir [or ma'am], you have to move." One day, I noticed a man looking at me in his rearview mirror as I drove up in the squad car alone, having dropped off Officer Johnson down the street. I waved at the man to indicate: "You have to go." He doesn't move. So I turned on my wigwags—that's what we called the flashing lights on the squad car. He still didn't move. Then I got out of the squad and walked toward his car. I noticed that his door was slightly ajar. I knew that seemed odd, and later I would be taught to watch out for this. But I was about to learn that lesson on my own, the hard way. As I approached his car, the man leaped out at me, knocking me to the ground. All of a sudden I found myself lying flat on the sidewalk amid the rush-hour bustle of departing office workers, with an agitated man on top of me. As I wrestled to get up, I spotted Officer Johnson, who was not in the best shape, running down the block toward us. He jumped on top of this man and together we finally got him hand-cuffed. Later we found out he was suffering from a mental health crisis after losing his job that day.

Once the man was safely in the back of the squad car, Officer Johnson apologized by saying, "I shouldn't have left you, kid." I knew he meant it. He was responsible for me, and I had been assaulted. He explained that he had been halfway down the block writing a ticket for an elderly woman when she interrupted, "Sir, Officer, I think there's something you need to be paying attention to." He looked in the direction she was pointing. Holy cow! The Boot was on the pavement! "Kid," he said, "I didn't give her a ticket."

That was my introduction to policing. In the end, I demonstrated enough good sense for Officer Johnson to sign off on me. I was no longer a Boot—I had joined the ranks as a patrol officer.

4

The Two Things Cops Hate Most

MY FIRST ASSIGNMENT AS A PATROL OFFICER WAS TO THE 4TH PRECINCT IN NORTH Minneapolis, where I would work for much of my career. One of the busiest precincts in the city, today the population of North Minneapolis is 82 percent people of color, 62 percent of whom are Black or African American. Nearly 35 percent speak a language other than English. About 35 percent of neighborhood residents are under the age of eighteen. The median household income in 2022 was just over $48,000.

The neighborhood residents, business owners, and workers got to know the neighborhood beat officers over time. Walking for eight hours a day—up Penn Avenue North to Golden Valley Road, pacing the entire stretch of GVR, as we called it in the precinct, and doubling back to Plymouth Avenue—was an incredible learning experience. I responded to everything from serious crimes to commonplace frictions. Walking a beat kept me in constant communication with residents raising their families on the North Side and with those who were causing problems. If I had to radio for a squad car, it meant I hadn't done my job. If a group of men playing dice and drinking beer outside were getting a bit rowdy, I would walk up to them and say, "You gotta go inside. I'm getting calls on this." I gave them a choice to avoid the squad car, and I gave their neighbors a little leverage. If the noisy dice players came back outside later when the next door neighbor was trying to put his kids to bed, he could say to them, "Officer Rondo told you all to take that inside." This would serve as a helpful reminder to the players, who were not trying to draw attention to themselves if they could avoid it. Day by day, as laws were enforced and shared expectations developed, we patrol officers played our part in the rhythm of neighborhood life.

Some days, however, routine gave way to heartache. During one patrol shift early in my career, I answered a "baby not breathing" call at 10:00 p.m. There are two calls police officers dread most: "officer down" and "baby not breathing." No other calls will make you move at such superhuman speed to respond. Nothing is sadder than when a "baby not breathing" call turns into a fatality, as it did that night. At 11:00 p.m. I moved on to a domestic abuse call where I tried to help a woman who had been badly beaten. By midnight, I was at the scene of a violent homicide. Three horrors in three hours. When I returned to the precinct, I sat in the roll call room trying to process what I had just experienced. It's not normal to see these things. It wounds your psyche. I needed to breathe. The sergeant spied me sitting down and came over. "What's up, kid?" he said. I told him about the calls and said I was taking a minute to regroup. His response was to kick my stool and say, "Suck it up, kid. Get back out there."

This scene still plays out in today's police culture. It simply has to end. We expect officers to go into the worst situations you can imagine—to encounter a vulnerable, unsheltered person living on the street in the most inhumane conditions, or a young person who's been sex trafficked—and we expect those same officers to "suck it up." I want to be candid with people entering this profession: Most of you will experience traumatic events that others never see. It will impact your mental health and wellness, and we need to talk about that. Leaders like me need to remove the stigma of trauma and depression and instill the necessity of mental health care. We can't just give officers training and a paycheck and call it good. The first time I ever sat down with a psychologist was for the mandatory pre-employment interview when I joined the department in 1989. That was also the last time—and that's not a good thing. It's not healthy to just stuff the trauma down and move on. If we don't do better, we're going to lose good people who wear the badge.

While there are days when we encounter society at its worst, or life at its hardest, most things police officers do during a shift are not monumental. That doesn't mean they're not significant. You never know what a small act of kindness will mean to someone. When I was walking down the street in my patrol uniform, I would sometimes see a child looking at me with wide eyes. I would greet her parents with a smile, take a bended knee so I could look the child in the eye, and say, "How are you?" A moment before, I had been a large, intimidating person in uniform, but a friendly hello made me approachable. I showed the child that I noticed her. I showed her parents that I have humility.

When community members know you to be approachable, reasonable, and fair, they will talk to you when it matters most. During my time as chief, budget and staffing shortages forced me to eliminate all foot beats. We had so few officers and so many 911 calls that everyone available was spending their shifts in squad cars, rushing from call to call. They had no time to listen to that elderly crime victim who just had a break-in and needed a few minutes to be reassured. Without the opportunity to provide comfort or to have consistent touchpoints with community members, the department lost opportunities to build trust.

In nine minutes in 2020, Derek Chauvin set Minneapolis policing back for a long, long time. When someone tarnishes the badge, it hurts all of us who wear the uniform. On May 15, 2021—about a year later—nine-year-old Trinity Ottoson-Smith was hit in the head by a stray bullet while jumping on a backyard trampoline with other children. I sat with her father at North Memorial Hospital, holding his hand at Trinity's bedside as we prayed for her survival. She died on May 27. Someone in the community knew the identity of the shooter. But not a single person came forward that summer. That is one consequence of distrust. The Minnesota Department of Public Safety offered a $180,000 Crime Stoppers reward, but I felt strongly that such an incentive should not be necessary to compel information. We should not hear crickets when children are slain. It took nearly a year to bring charges and even longer to convict the man who killed Trinity, a delay that compounded her family's suffering and prolonged the fear and unease in her neighborhood at the heart of the 4th Precinct.

At the time of Trinity's death, her neighborhood still bore the scars of decades of tension between the community and police. The older storefronts along the main street had been lost to fire during the 1967 protests. At the same time, the civil rights era had paved the way for a new center for Black arts and culture. The community center known as "The Way" was established in 1966. One of the few resources of its kind, The Way was a cultural hub for Black youth, offering sports, cultural events, and classes on Black history. Its rehearsal and performance spaces were a musical incubator for the famed Minneapolis Sound, supporting many local musicians—including a young Prince. After nearly two decades, however, The Way closed in 1984 in the face of ongoing funding challenges. In the mid-1980s, the building was demolished and replaced with the Minneapolis Police Department's 4th Precinct headquarters. It's hard to miss the implied symbolism when a site of African American cultural heritage is replaced by a police precinct.

The bland 1980s architecture of the 4th Precinct building has not stood the test of time. It could charitably be described as drab. A flagpole stands out front near the glass entryway to a cramped lobby with faded paint and battered furniture. It's always too hot in summertime. In winter, officers sit next to space heaters because it is freezing. The precinct is surrounded by a six-foot-high brick wall. A ten-foot gate guards the entrance to the officers' parking lot. For a building of great importance to the community, it is not inviting now, and never has been. The structure conveys: We stand alone.

In certain ways, this insular architecture mirrors the culture of policing. The nature of the job creates a unique bond among the men and women who are tasked day and night to take on responsibilities—and confront dangers—that most people would never choose to face.

If you haven't done the job, it's very difficult to get a full contextual understanding of it.

When expressed as collaboration, the bond among officers can have a positive impact on culture, performance, and morale. On the other hand, the same ingredients can come together to form an "us against them" dynamic based on the belief that nobody else understands us. Officers are most likely to circle the wagons when they feel that they are scrutinized unfairly or that their role is being attacked. Stress and burnout can make a bad situation even worse because policing is one of the few professions in the country where the workload is relentless but cannot be contracted out. Police officers have to show up every day, no matter what. There is no flexibility to bring in temps, dial back the pace, or give everyone the day off. You can't. You still have to respond to 911 calls.

Every officer must make a conscious decision about how they will position themselves within this close-knit culture. If you are an officer who wants to be part of the team while still living up to department values and practicing procedural justice, that's okay. If you define yourself entirely by the job, you will eventually find yourself at loose ends. All police are destined to become civilians again. There's not a single hundred-year-old officer working today.

Some people slowly discard the friends they had before they were on the job until their colleagues are their only friends. Once this happens, it makes it very difficult to speak out against the group. It's incumbent upon leaders to support new officers when they are at this crossroads, but in the end, it's a personal choice. Some will decide: "I'm part of the team and I'll always stay close. I'll be a good team player, even if that sometimes means going against my values or the department's policies." Others will decide: "I enjoy being a police officer; however, I'm going to be more independent in my career journey. I'm going to have friends who are colleagues but also keep a healthy number of friends who are not part of this profession. I'm not going to let the job define who I am."

These different paths can coexist within the culture of a police department. In my experience, the independent path is more difficult to follow because the culture is not designed for free thinkers. It's a paramilitary organization—a ranked structure where you take orders. Today, departments across the country, including

Minneapolis, are emphasizing the importance of individual officers using common sense and discretion at every stage of their career. For the past 150 years, however, this has not been the case.

I had chosen what type of officer I wanted to be before I even joined the MPD, but there were times when my resolution was put to the test. One was a hot day in September 1992, just three years into my career, when I was working mid-shift as a patrol officer in North Minneapolis. I was alone in my squad car when the dispatcher came on the radio: "Metro Transit just alerted us that a plainclothes transit officer is fighting with a man outside of a bus at the corner of Plymouth and Emerson Avenue N. He needs assistance."

I was just a few blocks away from the location when dispatch issued a tone-and-alert, which signals more squad cars to come. The situation was escalating. I turned my lights on and hit the gas. As I approached the intersection, I saw a city bus pulled over to the curb about fifty yards away from a community center called The City, Inc., where a lot of our Black youth gathered. The youth and staff from the community center had observed what was happening outside the bus and walked over. Other passersby had joined them. By the time I arrived, at least a hundred people had massed around the bus stop. A handful of white MPD officers made their way through the mostly Black crowd. I was the only Black officer on the scene.

A white, plainclothes Metro Transit officer stood on the sidewalk near the bus. By the time I arrived, he had been separated from the other person involved in the altercation. To my great surprise, that person was an elderly Black man who was also blind. I quickly learned what had taken place. The blind man had tried to board the bus but was a few cents short on the fare. The Metro Transit officer told him to get off the bus. The man pleaded to be let on the bus, explaining he was just trying to get downtown. The Metro Transit officer decided to respond by trying to physically remove this disabled Black senior citizen from the bus. As a result, both men fell into the street. Word of the officer's aggression and lack of compassion spread quickly through the crowd, and many were visibly upset. People began to shout their demands that the transit officer be held accountable for assaulting the elderly man. The officer's mistreatment of a vulnerable person would be inexcusable in any case, but it was especially insulting because the stakes were, literally, small change. Members of the crowd viewed the officer's actions as disrespectful and racially biased. For many in the community, this was an all-too-familiar example of a disproportionate response by a white officer to a minor infraction by a Black man.

I pushed my way through the throng of shouting, angry citizens and tried to calm the situation down. As I spotted North Side residents I recognized, I said, "Hey, can you tell me what's going on here?" It was no use. The tension had escalated to the verge of pandemonium. That's when I spotted my uncle, who I'll call Darren. He was a large, muscular Black man wearing a white tank top. He stood out in the crowd for his size and strength. At that moment, Uncle Darren was facing off against a white MPD officer. When the officer tried to place his hands on my uncle's wrists, they looked like a child's hands against the bulk of Uncle Darren's arms.

What happened next plays back in my memory like a slow motion video. I heard the N-word unfurl from the white officer's mouth: "nnniiiiii . . ." Simultaneously, I saw my uncle's closed fist swing toward the officer's face—word and action in collision. A hush came over the crowd when the N-word and my uncle's haymaker cut through the air. You could have heard a pin drop. A smacking crunch broke the silence as my uncle landed his punch.

Everyone knew something worse was going to happen next. But we didn't know what. The only certainty was that a white officer using a racial slur was not going to bring any sort of calm to the situation. We also knew Uncle Darren was definitely going to jail. He had just hit a police officer in front of a hundred people.

As soon as he heard an officer say "We gotta arrest him," Uncle Darren asserted, "The only way I'm getting in a squad car is if my nephew takes me." Then he pointed at me. In that moment, the supervising officer on the scene was given an opportunity to stop things from getting worse. He took it. "Rondo," he said, "you take him in." The other officers heard this order and they parted along with the crowd—giving me room to get through with my uncle. I believe everyone there in that moment realized how bad it could have gotten and accepted that this was probably the best outcome.

On the way to my squad car, my uncle said to me, "There's no way I was going to let him call me out of my name. I'm a man. I wasn't going to let him try to take my dignity away from me. If you hadn't been there, I wasn't going to let them take me downtown." He was afraid that if he got in the back of that squad car with the white officer, he was not going to make it to the jail.

The Metro Transit officer's assault, and subsequently the MPD officer's slur, provided receipts for many in the community who were discontented with policing and the MPD. From time to time I've been asked why I, as a Black man who is also a student of history, chose to join the profession in the first place. This scenario is one reason why. If we did not have Black individuals working for change within this broken system, how might this encounter have ended? I can tell you it would have ended badly for my uncle.

That evening, Police Chief John Laux and other city officials met with neighborhood residents at North High School. There were long-standing grievances to be discussed, but word had spread quickly about the afternoon assault on the blind, elderly Black man, and that was the residents' most urgent concern. I did not attend that meeting because I was still on my shift, but I know it did not go well. Many residents left angry and upset, feeling that their questions were unanswered and their concerns unheeded. Someone smashed a window on a squad car parked outside the school. What I observed most keenly in the city that day was the tension of young people. They were frustrated. They felt the police were just giving them lip service, and they weren't buying it. As the clock ticked past midnight in the hot and restless city, that unresolved tension led to a shocking tragedy.

Following the contentious meeting at North High School, members of the Vice Lords street gang decided to retaliate. One gang member later testified that they first considered shooting out the tires of city buses, in response to the treatment of the elderly Black man. Later, they changed their minds and decided to shoot a police officer. Vice Lords Amwati "Pepi" McKenzie, Shannon Bowles, Montery Willis, and A. C. Ford drove to the Pizza Shack in South Minneapolis. It was known to be a cops' hangout, where officers went on their meal breaks. Officer Jerome Haaf, a thirty-year veteran of the MPD, was sitting at the "officers' table" drinking coffee. He was the only uniformed officer there. The two gunmen, McKenzie and Bowles, walked inside and shot Officer Haaf multiple times in the back. All four gang members were later convicted of his murder and sentenced to life in prison. The murder of Officer Haaf is seared into the city's memory. His loss is still felt in the MPD today, even by officers who never had the chance to know him.

Several days later, with the city still on edge, my uncle Darren's case for fourth degree assault against an officer was sent to the county attorney's office. I was called to the Hennepin County Government Center. I was waiting for the assistant county attorney in the hallway when she walked over and said to me, "I just need to know. I need to know the truth. Did that white officer call the defendant the N-word?" I looked at her and I said yes. She stood for a moment looking at me sideways, as if she was taken aback. "Wait here," she said, and walked into her office. After several minutes, she came back out. "That's all I needed to know," she said. "I'm dismissing this case." My uncle Darren would not be prosecuted.

Shortly after that conversation, I ran into Keith Ellison, the young attorney who represented my uncle before his case was dismissed. It was the first time we met. He said, "Are you Rondo?" When I answered yes, he told me about his consultation with my uncle as they had prepared for his case to go to trial. Uncle Darren wanted to call me as a witness. Ellison said, "I told your uncle that there is no way a Black cop is going to speak out against this white officer. No way. Not if he wants to keep his job. But your uncle pleaded to get that assistant county attorney to ask you. He promised you would tell her what really happened. When she said you told the truth, I couldn't believe it."

Fifteen years later, when Ellison became the first Muslim elected to Congress and the first African American representative from Minnesota, he would find himself the target of an alleged slur from a police officer. MPD Lieutenant Bob Kroll was reported by fellow officers for labeling the congressman a terrorist. Ellison received an apology from the chief and the mayor.

I can understand why my truthful statement to the assistant county attorney surprised Ellison—but for my part, I couldn't imagine *not* telling the truth. There was no way I was going to lie.

Telling the truth is a simple rule to live by. I can't think of a profession where fidelity to the truth is more vital than in policing. But I didn't have to learn this in the police academy or from Officer Johnson. I learned it on Park Avenue from my parents.

We know that many of the systems we must navigate are broken, including the system of policing. But we are better off having people working toward change within these systems, as well as people working outside these systems. At a very early stage in my career I felt that I could try to be a conduit between the Black community and the police department. I'm a part of this community and I'm a part of this profession and maybe my role is to be a bridge. I felt needed in both places. I was not afraid to tell the truth, and I was not at all motivated to "go along to get along." I was also not intimidated. My determination had only been strengthened by a disturbing racist threat earlier that year of 1992.

I was working dogwatch on the North Side when the desk officer asked me to do the mail run for that shift. This was a nightly ritual. One of us would grab the empty mail pouch and drive to City Hall in a squad car to pick up the correspondence, court subpoenas, and other mail that had been sorted into locked slots, one for each precinct. That night, another Black officer named Alisa Clemmons rode downtown with me. When we got back to the precinct, she handed the full bag of mail to the desk officer, who began to sort through the letters and packages. He pulled out a brown envelope addressed to me and another envelope, the same size and color, addressed to Officer Clemmons. As he went through the mail pile, the desk officer realized that there was a brown envelope for every Black officer in the 4th Precinct—and only for the Black officers. He made an uneasy joke about it. "Huh. Don't I get a letter?"

Officer Clemmons and I opened our identical envelopes while standing at the front desk. We read the letters inside. I kept a copy of mine. It reads:

KKK

IT HAS BEEN BROUGHT TO OUR ATTENTION THAT YOU N____S HAVE BEEN MAKING DEMANDS FOR FAVORITISM WITHIN OUR ORGANIZATION. THERE ARE MANY MEMBERS OF THE K.K.K. THAT WORK WITHIN YOUR ESTABLISHMENT THAT HAVE BEEN REPORTING YOU [sic] BEHAVIOR AND WE ARE HERE TO TELL YOU THAT IT MUST STOP OR WE WILL STOP YOU! YOU N___S WILL HAVE TO BE TAUGHT A LESSON IF YOU DO NOT FOLLOW THIS ADVISE [sic]. YOU [sic] N___ ORGANIZATION WILL NOT SAVE YOU!

I looked at Officer Clemmons and I could immediately tell she had just read the same words. I saw devastation moving across her face. We shared the instant realization that there were no stamps on these letters. Only someone within the department could have placed these letters inside the secure mail room. The letter invoked the KKK to instill terror. Its delivery through internal channels signaled: We can get to you.

My family and community elders had tried to prepare me for a moment like this, but still I was shocked. They told me that if I chose to work toward change from within the MPD, I was going to experience the brokenness of that organization. "Just be ready," they said. But it's one thing to know that history repeats itself, and quite another to experience it firsthand.

I felt sad—and outraged. I thought, "How dare you!" Standing at the front desk, Officer Clemmons and I tried to process what was happening. We knew that the Black officers had only tried to improve the organization—yet this was how some of our colleagues felt about us. This letter was telling us that we didn't belong. Soon, however, a kind of alchemy occurred as my feelings of pain and frustration transformed into a fortifying sense of resolve. I didn't know who sent the letter, but it was within my power to show them it would not have the effect they intended.

The desk officer contacted the sergeant on the radio. The sergeant made a call to the precinct inspector who was at home sleeping. Within hours, the chief and the mayor were aware of the letters and the FBI was notified of this threat to our lives. The FBI seized the unopened letters, which turned out to be all the same. Their agents conducted a full-blown investigation, including forensics. They removed the ribbons from electric typewriters to trace the letter's origin and conducted interviews across the organization.

At the time, the Minneapolis Black Officers Association had recently been formed, and I believe that is the "N-word organization" referred to in the letter. The goal of the association was for senior Black officers to give guidance and support to younger Black officers. It was a way to build fellowship and to help us navigate our careers. Clearly the letter writer, or writers, noticed that for the first time Black officers, who were (and still are) a small percentage of the rank and file, were starting to organize. We were questioning the way things had always been done—and in doing so, we were a threat to the way of life in the MPD.

I understood that the people behind the letter were watching what the Black officers would do. The letter was a "shock and awe" tactic meant to intimidate us into backing down or leaving the department altogether. So I made sure that my demeanor in the precinct was completely consistent with what it had been the day before the letters arrived. When anyone asked me how I was holding up, I told them, "I'm good. I'm not going anywhere." This doesn't mean I shut down my feelings. Neither was it a false front. I simply realized that part of their play was to hit us with so much distress that psychological paralysis would shut us down—and that would be a win for whoever wrote the letter.

Not a single Black officer left the department in response to that letter. Some of the veteran Black officers were not that surprised by the threat. They seemed to accept that it was what it was. If you know the history, you realize that sometimes bad things happen. As horrible as that hate mail was, I was able to draw upon the experience to build bridges to the Black community because I knew, to some degree, what it felt like to be targeted because of your race.

I didn't tell any of my family members what happened, except my father. I gave him a copy of the letter and said, "I want you to hold onto this, in the event anything should happen to me." He said, "I'm here for you," and, understanding the gravity of the threat, "Watch yourself."

The night that every Black officer received hate mail was also the night that Minneapolis hosted the 1992 Super Bowl. As football fans from around the country gathered for America's game, MPD officers provided security at the stadium. The television broadcasts showcased Minneapolis as a thriving metropolis, a progressive Northern star city. But behind the scenes at the precinct, our city's progressive reputation was being put to the test. In the end, the FBI investigation closed without identifying any suspects. The MPD administration moved on without a single policy change, memo, or other acknowledgment that the letters might signal a deep cultural problem.

Nevertheless, the letter may have had an unintended consequence. It became harder to brush aside discrimination complaints from citizens when our own officers were experiencing racial intimidation. It would be twenty-six years before Minneapolis hosted another Super Bowl. I will never know who wrote the letters, but I hope it was not lost on them that when the 2018 Super Bowl came to Minneapolis, I—someone they called a n———r and threatened—was the chief of police.

Over the next fifteen years, I and other Black officers continued to battle discrimination within the MPD. I took part in many discussions and negotiations with the administration. But I felt that I was having too many of the same conversations with younger Black officers in the 2000s that I'd had in meetings of the Black Officers Association back in 1992. Systemic change was needed—and so were new and bolder tactics. We were trying to repair a house with a rotting frame. You can bring in new paint and dazzle up the inside but it's not a real solution because the structure is not sound. You must get down to the studs to change what's underneath. For too many years, the department had only been coating over the walls and moving around the furniture.

In 2007, I joined four other Black officers in suing the Minneapolis Police Department for racial discrimination. Lieutenant Donald Harris, Sergeant Charles Adams, Sergeant Dennis Hamilton, Lieutenant Lee Edwards, and I were represented by Minneapolis attorney John Klassen.

It was a turning point for both the department and for those of us within the organization who felt an obligation to create progress. We took aim at the pattern of discrimination that stalled or set back the careers of Black officers. Our goal was to make things better for the younger officers coming up behind us. Although our lawsuit centered on Black officers, the reforms we sought would also benefit women, LGBTQ officers, and all people of color. We contested practices that resulted in missed opportunities for the department to capitalize on the value of its diversity. We wanted to improve the MPD, and we felt the need to bring this problem to the attention of the city.

It landed with a splash on the front page of the *Minneapolis Star Tribune*. At that time, I was the lieutenant in charge of the North Side Community Response Team (CRT), a dedicated group of plainclothes officers who worked on drug crimes and livability issues in the neighborhood. There were no other Black officers in the unit. There was some initial awkwardness when I arrived at the precinct the morning the news broke. I picked up a newspaper off a nearby desk, held it up, and addressed the unit. I wanted them to hear about the lawsuit from me in person, not from the rumor mill and not in an email. I said, "I want everyone to know this is an employment-related matter and we're going to let this process play out. This lawsuit is trying to improve the organization because it's broken in many places. However, it doesn't change the fact that I will continue to support the great work you're doing out there. The community needs you and they're depending on you. I don't want this to become a distraction. Let's get to work." When the CRT officers saw that I was going to treat them the same way I always had, they felt comfortable treating me the same way, too—and so we were able to concentrate on our work.

This lawsuit was unique in the sense that the facts were never disputed. This was not litigation meant to shame and hurt the organization—it was just the opposite. Our goal was to bring awareness to a historical situation that was not in the hands of one person in particular, but was meant to address decades-old, department-wide problems. That's why our lawsuit focused on policy—because policy changes, if done right, can outlive individuals within the organization. Our purpose was to call out and correct discrimination against African Americans in MPD hiring and promotion practices, training and education, work assignments, discipline, and overtime compensation.

That said, a broken organization can have broken individuals. Some of our contemporaries were specifically named in the lawsuit—most notably Lieutenant Bob Kroll, who had a notorious reputation in the community based on his history of racially discriminatory statements and conduct. Kroll was not subtle in his attitude and was alleged to signal his stance by wearing a motorcycle jacket with a "white power" patch.

The lawsuit resulted in a $740,000 settlement against the city and led to crucial reforms. One of the most significant outcomes was an overhaul of the process of "detailing" officers to interim positions of a higher rank. For example, if a sergeant leaves the department and needs to be replaced immediately, the chief can detail an officer to that position while searching for a permanent replacement. The detailed officer, despite not holding the civil service rank required for the role, will be temporarily bumped up to sergeant, with increased pay. This is considered a valuable opportunity for career advancement, and often the detailed officer will be selected to retain the promotion permanently, if they take the civil service exam.

There is a process for building and managing the pipeline of officers who are ready to advance to a higher rank. Officers wishing to be promoted take a qualifying exam and their names go on a list, ranked according to their test scores and work experience. However, the administration was detailing white officers who were lower on the promotion list than Black officers. Sometimes it detailed officers who were not on the list at all. The designated path to advancement was cut off for Black officers while work-arounds were used to advance white officers instead. The continued detailing of less qualified white officers, when combined with the non-consideration of equally qualified Black officers, had the effect of creating an almost exclusively white command structure. The lawsuit applied pressure to end these work-arounds, giving Black officers a fairer chance to be promoted on their merit according to their test scores and experience. If you don't call it out, it doesn't change. But changing a culture is more challenging than changing a policy—and it takes time. The two things cops hate most are change and the way things are.

I always tried to help younger officers when I could, because they were the ones who would carry changes forward long after I was gone. One day when I was working as a lieutenant in the 4th Precinct, a recruit I'll call Teresa Simpson walked past the open door of my office. She was a young Black woman who had some family members that were known to the police (as I did, too, like my uncle Darren). Simpson had grown up in Minneapolis. She knew that the residents and officers of the 4th Precinct faced a lot of challenges. She understood that the job would be difficult and stressful. But I could see in her face that she was struggling. I called out and invited her to step into my office. She was surprised when I asked her how her training was going. She said, "I'm having a bad day. I don't think they want me here."

No matter what journey I have experienced as a Black man in the profession, I can't even begin to fathom what it's like for a woman of color. But I can be an advocate and a mentor. I can be a truthsayer. I can share what I know about the pitfalls, challenges, and land mines that female officers may encounter—but also point out the rewards. "The work will be difficult and there will be setbacks,"

I said to Teresa Simpson. "But I can tell you from experience that when you reach your goal, you will appreciate the struggle that got you there." I saw the determination in Teresa Simpson. I told her, "You're going to make it, and if anyone gives you a hard time, you let me know." Years later, I encouraged her to take the sergeant's exam. I particularly encouraged officers of color to take that test. I knew that, because of how Officer Simpson had been treated as a recruit, if she became a supervisor she would never treat someone else that way. Today, Simpson leads department-wide training with an emphasis on procedural justice.

To my knowledge, there have never been more than a dozen Black women at one time in the Minneapolis Police Department. Simpson is one of a very few Black women who have ever made it to such a high command position in a culture where some still believe that people of color, and certainly Black women, were never meant to be leaders. But Simpson never gave up. She ignored the naysayers, and no matter what challenges she faced along the way, she has never lost sight of the value she brings to the department.

5

The Two-Year Itch

SOME POLICE OFFICERS DETERMINE EARLY IN THEIR CAREERS THAT THEY ARE meant to be patrol officers—it suits them, they're good at it, and they want to retire as a patrol officer. Others may decide that they want to climb the ranks, so they chart a course up the ladder. I was more of a wanderer—always seeking out where I fit within the organization. My career path was unorthodox because every two years or so I took on a new assignment. It might not have been the most glamorous assignment, but I took it if I could serve my community in a different way and if it allowed me to learn something new.

I've always been fascinated with leaders throughout history, including private sector leaders. I've met with many CEOs. All of them, to a person, have told me that they didn't consider themselves subject matter experts. Rather, they were generalists who surrounded themselves with great teams. On their path to leadership, these CEOs developed in-depth knowledge of how their organizations worked because of the varied positions they had held. Most of them were not linear in their path. While I didn't know this when I was a curious young officer trying to make my way through the MPD, I believe in retrospect that my "two-year itch" served me well as a leader. None of my various roles were undertaken with a mindset that the end goal was to become the chief. That was just how it came to be.

I've observed that when someone makes it known that their number one goal is to get to the top, many of their relationships become transactional. There was never a time I felt that I used somebody. There was never a time I felt that I owed somebody. When I did become chief, no one knocked on my door with something held over my head.

I had been embedded in all four corners of the organization from patrol work to investigations, from working plainclothes to drafting policy. The chief's office is several layers removed from the folks who are answering 911 calls or the investigators at crime scenes—but even though I was no longer out stringing up crime-scene tape or walking an application for a search warrant to a judge late at night, I had done it all.

Of the many positions I held through the years, a few stand out as foundational. These roles taught me to stay grounded in my duty to serve and showed me what happens when an officer's values or judgment fall out of alignment with the principles of our profession. The first is my combined time as an investigator and, later, as commander of the internal affairs unit responsible for investigating police misconduct. The second is my assignment as a school resource officer working on behalf of young people in our community.

From 1994 to 1996, I was the school resource officer at Franklin Middle School in North Minneapolis. Today there is debate over the role of school resource officers. A common and understandable concern is the potential for school resource officers to introduce students into the criminal justice system by issuing citations for conduct that would otherwise be handled by school staff. On the other hand, national research also shows that selecting the right officers, with the right values and training, reduces truancy—keeping kids in the classroom where they are learning. Reducing truancy also reduces the number of calls to report misbehavior by kids who are skipping school. In Minneapolis we have had many exemplary school resource officers who have been successful coaches for our youth—both in the hallways and on the athletic fields. The daily presence of a trusted officer, who is part of an ecosystem of student support, provides an opportunity to have conversations with young people who might wonder: "What is your job about? I've got a perception that you cause harm—but is that what I see here?"

During my two years as a school resource officer—and through my own experiences as a parent—I saw that while kids might not like being disciplined when it happens, they ultimately need and want a caring adult to provide an appropriate safeguard when they're going off the rails. It shows kids we believe they are capable of doing better. I was able to assist kids in resolving small conflicts before they became big problems—often by giving students the tools to negotiate disputes themselves.

School resource officers are in a unique position to understand that schools are an extension of our community and that students carry a lot on their shoulders. Many of the students at Franklin Middle School faced significant challenges and hardships in their daily lives. School was an oasis of caring adults who believed in a student's ability to succeed. On occasion, however, the learning environment we strove to create could be disrupted by dynamics brought from outside the classroom. That's when I could often help.

One day I got a call from the main office on my school-issued walkie-talkie. It was just after sunrise on a cold winter morning when the snow tracked in on the kids' boots was beginning to melt in the hallways. The school secretary asked me to stop by Mrs. D's seventh-grade math class because she was reporting an unruly student. Dressed in a sport coat and wearing my badge on a lanyard, I walked into the classroom during the first period, around 7:45 a.m. I asked Mrs. D what seemed to be the problem. She pointed to an African American boy who was probably twelve or thirteen years old. She said, "I don't like his demeanor. I believe he's involved in a gang." I replied, "Well, you don't like his demeanor, but what is he doing that is disrupting the class?" She repeated her belief about the student's gang affiliation. And I repeated back to her, "Well, Mrs. D, if he does something that rises to the level of being disruptive, please let me know." Then I left. I know she was not happy with my response.

The next day, I received another call from the office and I went to Mrs. D's classroom a second time. I asked Mrs. D what the problem was today. She pointed to the same boy and said, "I don't want gang members in my class." How did she know he was a gang member, I inquired. It turned out she had asked him. "Okay," I said. "He told you this because you asked him. But what's he doing to disrupt the class?" Then I requested that Mrs. D step into the hallway with me. Out of earshot of the students I spoke candidly, as an officer to an educator. "If that young man is making a daily decision that school is still important enough for him to get up before dawn to stand at a freezing bus stop in this frigid winter weather and then sit at his desk all through your boring class, it is your responsibility to teach him," I said. "So teach him."

I was expressing my view of what Mrs. D had signed up for: to do her best to make sure her students were learning in the school environment. As a police officer, I felt that if a student was in a gang and there was a way to give him opportunities other than that gang, we had to meet him halfway. This student was already meeting us halfway by showing up to Mrs. D's classroom every morning, but Mrs. D's complaints were sure to undermine the boy's resolve by sending a message that he was unworthy to be there.

In that instance, I felt Mrs. D had fallen short. But I have a great deal of respect for teachers and an affinity for the work they do for our children. Parents entrust their children's care and protection to a group of adults at school who they may never know. Parents trust that these educators and staff are teaching their children properly, monitoring their social interactions, and reinforcing important social expectations like taking turns, being good listeners, and treating others respectfully. I would have trusted my own children at Franklin Middle School any day of the week—and that was due in large part to the leadership of Mrs. Purvis, the vice principal. Mrs. Purvis believed wholeheartedly in the limitless potential of her students and let the children know that they could achieve their dreams. She knew every student by name and always greeted her staff with a friendly smile. She could be a disciplinarian when she had to, and she did not suffer fools. At six feet tall, she was an imposing presence. Mrs. Purvis watched out for her students and, as it turned out, she watched out for me, too.

The last day of school was a beautiful day in June. When the bell rang, teachers and staff walked outside with the students to the row of yellow buses lined up along the curb. We always made sure the students left the school safely, but we knew that on the last day of school kids could be a little rambunctious, so we were all paying special attention.

I was walking along the curb as the children boarded the buses, and Mrs. Purvis was about halfway down the block. All of a sudden, a vehicle pulled up and stopped in the middle of the street. The doors popped open as three women jumped out of the car and ran straight onto one of the buses. I looked at the bus driver and saw that he was waving at me to get over to that bus, *now.*

As I walked through the open door and up the stairs of the bus, I heard the women shouting loud profanities. These three adults were standing in the aisle yelling at a sixth- or seventh-grade girl. They were accusing this student of having some kind of conflict with one of their daughters. They were calling her out and it was clear they wanted to fight this young girl. I marveled to myself: "With all the problems that these kids are facing day to day, you three grown adults are going to come up here and act this way?" There was no way I was going to let them drag that child off the bus. I immediately identified myself as the school resource officer and directed them very sternly to get out.

As I got all three women off the bus, I was trying to appeal to their common sense—if they had any. I said, "You can't be doing this!" That's when one of the women started to circle around behind me and I thought: "Oh no. This is probably not going to go well." Sure enough, before I could make a move, she jumped on my back. My walkie-talkie flew off as she began punching me while the other two women piled on, fists flying. They had come looking for a fight, and now they were going to fight me. All I could think was: "There are buses full of kids watching this. I do not want to engage in a scuffle with these women in view of the children."

I worked without a partner officer, but that day Mrs. Purvis showed up as my partner. As I was standing there getting pummeled while trying to figure out what to do, I remember hearing Mrs. Purvis's voice cut straight through the rumbling of the idling buses: "Oh no!" she roared. "You ain't about to be fighting Officer

Rondo!" Before I knew it, all six feet of Mrs. Purvis had pulled that woman off my back and she was grabbing the other two to get them off me. Not only that, but she had radioed the office to have them call for backup! Squad cars quickly arrived and arrested the women for assault.

Mrs. Purvis looked at me, taking in my torn blazer and slightly stunned expression, and I was surprised to see her so emotional. She was so concerned about me. We looked after each other at Franklin, and her actions were a response that let all the students and staff know that we're part of a family and what those three women did was not setting a proper example.

I told her, "I'm going to be just fine. Unfortunately I've been tackled by people jumping out of cars before."

Sometimes, school is the safest environment that kids experience, which is why I was so disappointed when, in the week following George Floyd's murder, the Minneapolis Public School District swiftly revoked resource officers from the schools. I felt that I had been able to make a difference at Franklin. Of all the bridges I have tried to build between the MPD and the community, the relationship with our young people is among the most important.

While my time as a school resource officer was one of the most outward-facing roles I held, my time as an investigator and commander in internal affairs was the most inward-facing. Internal affairs is the gatekeeper for police accountability. Typically, officers do not apply for a position in this unit. Instead, they are sought out based on character, integrity, and investigational skills. Movies and television shows depict internal affairs investigators as being shunned by other officers. They're the narcs. This was not my experience. Rather, it was typically considered a prestigious assignment because officers wanted to know that if they or their unit were investigated, it would be a fair, thorough, and impartial process. Internal affairs officers are fact-finders. Only the chief can issue discipline.

When misconduct has been proven, the offending officer must be held accountable, and that starts with their supervisor. The number one role of a supervisor is to mentor and provide support to improve the performance of his or her officers. Addressing a small problem when it occurs can often prevent a larger problem from developing. As a chief, I relied heavily on my frontline supervisors, who had their fingers on the pulse of the precincts day and night. They were in place to notice the earliest signs of trouble. Police officers are not immune to aging parents, children who are struggling, a cancer diagnosis, or other stressors that accompany us into the precinct and out on our shifts. This profession also has high rates of alcoholism and divorce. Life challenges both compound and reflect the occupational stress unique to our profession. The Centers for Disease Control reports that occupational stress in first responders is associated with increased risk of mental health issues, including hopelessness, anxiety, depression, and post-traumatic stress, as well as suicidal ideation and suicide attempts. When officers are suffering, we need to connect them with treatment and resources that can help, and we need to remove the stigma around it.

Supervisors are entrusted to give proper instruction, guidance, training, and discipline to their subordinates. When they fail to do this, they can destabilize the department's foundation and ruin the trust we have built with those we serve. There is sometimes a notion that by turning a blind eye or refusing to discipline an employee, a supervisor is somehow helping them—but they're not. By the time a misconduct case landed on my desk as an investigator, it was almost always evident that this employee had not just, out of the blue, started acting inappropriately. Supervisors were aware and saw poor behavior building up, but failed to intervene. In doing so, they forfeited a chance to save that officer's job.

If supervisors don't correct bad behavior, it will come to a head when someone out there in the community attempts to do it. In this profession that means a complaint, a lawsuit, a trial, or worse—a prison sentence. When that happens, the chief and the public will rightfully ask: Didn't anyone notice? Why didn't anyone put a stop to it? The stakes are too high for supervisors to be passive or hesitant to make tough decisions.

The case of former officer David Campbell is among the saddest and most shocking examples of what can happen when nobody speaks up. Campbell, age sixty, was a twenty-six-year veteran of the MPD when he was convicted in 2018 of criminal sexual conduct. He had been kicked out of his house and was living in a camper in the parking lot of the 2nd Precinct. This alone signaled a problem. But there were many more red flags. An internal affairs investigation found repeated incidents of showing up to work late, a disheveled appearance, excessive part-time work, use of profanity, and making threats against community members— resulting in multiple complaints against him.

During this time, Campbell took a teenage girl on ride-alongs in his squad car, where some of the incidents of sexual abuse occurred. She was his son's sixteen-year-old girlfriend. When Campbell was seen with her in the precinct, somebody should have asked questions about what was going on. Police officers are trained to ask questions. Where was the officer who said, "Excuse me? Who's this? Is this your daughter? No? Young lady, how old are you? What is your connection to him?"

Did nobody question this strange pairing of a young teenager and a scruffy adult man who lived in the parking lot? Campbell drove his victim around in a squad car—ignoring or skirting the policies that govern ride-alongs. Did nobody in the precinct notice this infraction? I believe someone did notice these problems, but they didn't act on them. Bad cops should never find refuge with their own peers, ever. We don't help our own people by turning a blind eye. I've never seen anything good come from that. Even worse, we inflict compound trauma on the victim. This sixteen-year-old girl was the victim of a crime. She suffered in silence before the very eyes of the people who were supposed to help her. We let her down.

The girl eventually sought help from a school social worker, prompting an investigation. I immediately suspended Campbell without pay. When the investigating agency from another jurisdiction arrested him, they alerted our department. As soon as I was notified that one of my officers had been booked into Hennepin County Jail for criminal sexual conduct with a minor, I terminated his employment. I had my internal affairs investigators walk over to the Hennepin County jail and hand-deliver his termination papers.

There is a culture in policing, just as there is in some families, that dictates: We don't air our dirty laundry. If Dad's got a drinking problem, we keep that in-house. If Junior has a problem in school, we keep that in-house. But that's unhealthy. If we circle the wagons, not only does it eventually harm us, but it can cause other people to suffer. I don't know why David Campbell, who was obviously not a high-performing officer in the first place, was given a pass or why his misdeeds were overlooked by his peers and supervisor. But I do know where they went wrong. First, when in doubt—when that nagging question appears in the back of your mind—don't dismiss it because it makes you uncomfortable. All sworn officers took an oath to serve the people, so officers must continually ask themselves: Who does this action—or inaction—serve? Second, Campbell's peers failed to accept their own responsibility for holding their fellow officer accountable. Every officer shares this responsibility equally—it's not confined to supervisors but applies to every officer of every rank. Failure to intervene in abuses of power has enormous consequences, as Tou Thao, J. Alexander Kueng, and Thomas Lane would discover when they stood by and watched George Floyd die.

6

A Badge Is Not a Shield

I SPENT MORE THAN THREE DECADES IN LAW ENFORCEMENT AND IT NEVER GOT EAS-
ier to break the news to a parent, sibling, spouse, or child that a loved
one had died. But there was a time it got even harder.

The evening of March 10, 2012, was a Saturday night with no
snow on the ground—unusual for that time of year in Minnesota.
Police officers are like meteorologists who become good at taking
the temperature of the city and forecasting how busy a shift will be.
Sometimes, this means literally checking the weather. Unlike the
saying, March usually *comes in* like a lamb and *goes out* like a lion in
Minnesota. So when a warm, mild evening draws people outside, restless from long months of winter, we know it's going to be a busy night.

I was a lieutenant at the time and the lead supervisor that night
for the 4th Precinct. I liked to lead by example, so I'd usually get
in my patrol vehicle to monitor calls or back up officers at calls. In
the late-night hours, as Saturday turned to Sunday, a call came in
for a shooting at a house on Emerson Avenue North. I put on lights
and sirens and drove up to the front of the house within minutes.

Minneapolis fire crews were already on scene. Several people stood outside the house. I heard a woman crying. I noticed more people along the side of the house, so I turned on my flashlight and walked in that direction.

As I entered the backyard, a woman came up to me in tears. She said, "Jason's been shot." I didn't recognize her, but I knew she was speaking to me personally—not as a witness addressing an officer. It seemed as if she were trying to console me, and I was reminded that the badge doesn't shield you from violence when it comes to your door.

I saw firefighters kneeling over a man who was lying face-up on the ground. They seemed to be performing CPR. I walked closer until my flashlight illuminated the man's face. I saw then that it was my younger cousin, Jason Youngmark. Jason was thirty-three years old, married, and the father of seven children. He had been shot in the chest. How had this come to be?

Soon the paramedics arrived and joined the firefighters, like a fine-tuned orchestra. They were doing all they could to provide lifesaving care to my cousin. I knew time was of the essence. He wasn't in that backyard long before he was sped by ambulance to North Memorial Hospital. Sadly, I've gone to a lot of shooting scenes. You can sometimes gauge the severity of the injury from the urgency and tone of the firefighters and paramedics. As the paramedics prepared to transport Jason, I knew it didn't look good. Nevertheless, our excellent and extremely capable emergency medical service teams—and the doctors and nurses at North Memorial Hospital and Hennepin County Medical Center (HCMC)—are the reason many gunshot victims are still walking around Minneapolis today.

Knowing Jason was in good hands, I kept hope in my heart as I gathered my wits and shifted my focus to the crime scene. Years of experience kicked in and penetrated my confusion and worry. I started asking the fundamental questions. "Is the suspect still here? Where is the weapon?" What struck me as unusual about the scene was the sadness that hung over the yard. This was not a chaotic scene with yelling and confrontation, as it so often is. This was a gathering of friends where something had gone horribly wrong. The witnesses did not flee the scene or refuse to cooperate. They knew who the shooter was, and they told me his name immediately. We had the weapon, because the shooter had dropped the gun before he ran off.

I stayed while the officers preserved the scene to prevent evidence from contamination. The detectives gathered witnesses' information so they could conduct further interviews down at City Hall. I was in my squad car on the way back to the precinct when a call came over the radio, addressing me by my squad number. Dispatch said, "401, can you give me a call?" I knew this meant she had something to say but she didn't want to say it on a public channel. When I called her back, she told me that Jason had been pronounced dead at the hospital.

I went back to my office and shut the door. I sat at my desk to make the call that nobody wants to make. It's never good when you have to break the news that will turn someone's life upside down. I've done it in the street, when family members rush to the scene wondering if the victim is their loved one. I've done it in the ER waiting room. Being born and raised in the city, I've lost friends to violence. But this was even worse.

Of course, my uncle would need to be notified—but I thought it was best for him to hear the news from my cousin Jermar, who was Jason's brother. Jermar and I are as close as brothers ourselves, and I knew I had to be the one to tell him. I recall telling Jermar that the EMS teams did everything they could to try to save Jason. I told him there were several witnesses to the shooting and that a suspect was known. I would keep him updated every step of the way. I ended the call with "I love you, cuz." It was an emotional call for both of us. But having to share in a moment of deep pain and grief can bring you closer, and it has for us in a profound way.

How do you explain the sudden loss of a man who had so much energy, love, and spirit? Jason was funny and kind. He would give you the shirt off his back. Above all, he was a family man, devoted to his wife and kids. He was taken from them by Ike Wilson Jr., a childhood friend who had followed a very different path in life. Jason had married, trained as an electrician, and started a business. Wilson was a four-time felon. He ultimately pleaded guilty to manslaughter and was sentenced to seventy-two months in prison.

When I look back at that day in 2012, I still think about the young woman who took it upon herself to tell me the terrible news, so that I would hear it from a sympathetic person. She created a space for me to begin to process a terrible shock. Even in her own grief, this woman was looking out for me. I think that's what we must all do. We as a Black community have to do a better job of looking out for one another.

For too many years, the majority of victims of gun violence and the majority who have pulled the trigger look like me. In Minneapolis, 83 percent of shooting victims are Black, according to MPD data for 2022. The data also show that 89 percent of shooting suspects are described as Black, in cases where suspect descriptions were provided. If we, as a community, don't address these two facts, we will extinguish the flame of hope for future generations. We must be willing to engage in tough but necessary conversations at home and in the public sphere. We must collectively face hard truths and confront the trauma that results when senseless violence is reaped upon our community.

When it comes to gun violence, the disparity between Blacks and whites is staggering. In 2021, there was one Black shooting victim for every 150 Black residents of Minneapolis. Compare those odds to the metric for white residents: In the same year, there was one white shooting victim for every 3,768 white residents. Now imagine if we discovered that one in 150 Black people in the city were diagnosed with cancer every year. There would be a massive public health effort to bring those numbers down. In fact, leaders of ten health care systems in Minnesota declared gun violence a public health emergency in 2022. We are losing a generation of young people to preventable deaths, and many who survive gunshot wounds bear serious physical and emotional scars. The vast majority of those killed or injured are young Black men.

Meanwhile, the perpetrators of gun violence are also lost to the community through prison terms. What is it like for their children to grow up without a father? We all pay the price for gun violence.

I chose to share this painful story about my cousin Jason because it's a reminder of how fragile life is. Jason had so much going for him. He was a loving father, taken from us before his thirty-fourth birthday. Our family tries to heal from his loss—but it never goes away. A parent outliving their child goes against the natural order of things. Jason is survived by his father, and I can only imagine what this loss has meant for my uncle. Because we are a large, yet close-knit family, Jason's widow and children have the support of cousins, aunts, uncles, in-laws, and grandparents who love them. But there will always be an empty space in the center of their home.

I believe Jason would not want his children to be sad for him, but instead to celebrate his life. His children are his legacy. Their mother, Stacy Davis, has nurtured, loved, and guided them every step of the way. Now ages thirteen to twenty-five, Jason and Stacy's children are a caring, vibrant group of siblings who have grown into a young athlete, a quiet observer who takes in everything around him, a caretaker of friends and siblings, a well-rounded student, a computer whiz, a leader of the pack, and a free spirit who works outdoors. Through each of them, Jason lives on.

If I could give anything to Jason's children in his absence, it would be the knowledge that they are worthy. I have always tried to instill this knowledge in my own children. I wanted to make sure that my kids knew that there was no replacing them. To this day, when I ask my adult son or daughter how they are doing, their response is typically, "I'm blessed and highly favored."

I believe one of the reasons we are losing Black lives is because we don't love each other. We can make a difference when we truly value one another. Along my journey I have experienced the life-changing impact that positive Black adult males and loving Black fathers have in the lives of Black boys and young Black men. My own father and uncles taught me to never have hate in my heart. As guardians of our community, adult Black men are an incredible force with the ability to pierce through a harmful social veneer that has, in recent generations, deceived young Black men with the notion that love weakens you, hope is a fantasy, and the only time that matters is today. What kind of future might our youth be empowered to build if we could confront and destroy that false narrative?

While positive Black men can provide an uplifting road map for the journey of our young men and boys, we *must* give our flowers to Black mothers who, through the ages, have endured so much and yet loved so much in helping to raise their children and make their dreams a reality.

There are many phenomenal leaders within the Minneapolis Black community and among our allies who have been working for generations to create positive change in the lives of Black people in this city. But the historical record in Minnesota shows that while advances have been made overall, Black Minnesotans still face huge disparities in education, housing, employment, and health.

I believe Black people have to be the ones to develop and administer the vaccine that will end the epidemic of violence. I believe we hold the answer. And that's a call to action. I'm willing to sit with Black leaders in business, health care, education, social work, faith communities, or anyone else who wants to make a change, because we've got to address this. The gun violence statistics have not fundamentally changed for decades. Like anything that's repetitive, people become desensitized to violence—and that's a crime in and of itself.

7

To Move Heaven and Earth

I WAS THE ASSISTANT CHIEF OF THE MINNEAPOLIS POLICE DEPARTMENT ON July 15, 2017—second-in-command under Chief Janeé Harteau. It had been a long day for me at the office. I walked out of City Hall into the kind of beautiful, cool summer night when you leave your windows open to enjoy the fresh air. I had just arrived home and was upstairs changing out of my work uniform when my phone rang. It was the watch commander. Whenever he called me after 11:30 p.m., I knew it was urgent. He is the chief of the night when all the other chiefs are at home. "AC," he said, "we just had an officer-involved shooting."

I slipped my arms back into the sleeves of my uniform shirt as I asked for more information. Where did this happen? Who's deceased? The location was an alley in a residential neighborhood with a very low crime rate, and the victim was female. This was out of the ordinary. I told the watch commander I'd be on the scene within fifteen minutes and then I called my boss. I was running point that night because Chief Harteau was away on vacation. She didn't answer her phone, so I left a short but detailed message. My next call was to inform her boss, Mayor Betsy Hodges.

When I arrived at the location, the crime-scene tape was already up. Yellow strips blocked the entrance to a dark alley that was lit up in blue and red by the flashing lights of the squad cars. I'm used to making my way to a crime scene through the hubbub of a gathering crowd or a cluster of reporters. But this scene was quiet and deserted. The duty officer logged my name and badge number and admitted me to walk past the tape into the stillness of the alley. Between two rows of tidy garages, I saw the figure of the deceased lying with her back on the pavement, her face pointed toward the night sky. She was a white woman with blonde hair, around forty years old, barefoot, and dressed in pajamas. It was evident that the cause of death was a gunshot wound to the abdomen.

The deceased woman lay just a few feet from the driver's side of a parked Minneapolis squad car. She had been facing the car when she was shot, and had fallen backward. What stood out to me immediately was that the driver's-side door was shut, with the window rolled down. The passenger-side door, on the opposite side of the car from the victim, was fully open.

When the watch commander and a detective on scene walked over to me, I asked whether we had identified which of the two patrol officers had fired the fatal shot. It was the passenger officer, Mohamed Noor, age thirty-one, a Somali American who had joined the department just under two years before. Noor had been riding that night with his partner, twenty-five-year-old Matthew Harrity, who was driving the squad.

My mind was struggling to figure out how the officer sitting in the passenger seat had shot a person standing outside the car on the driver's side. Police officers complete extensive firearms training, so my thoughts went first to a scenario that we have trained for. If the officer saw a threat coming from the driver's side of the parked car, he may have opened his passenger-side door, rounded outside the door, and used the hood of his car to shield and steady himself to fire at the threat. However, that notion didn't line up with other evidence at the scene.

"AC," said the detective, "what we have here is the passenger officer fired his weapon from inside the squad car, out the driver's-side window." This scenario made even less sense. Where was Harrity, the driver, when the shot was fired? Was he out on foot? "No," said the detective. "Harrity was in the car."

What on earth could have caused a police officer to unholster and fire his gun from inside his vehicle, past his partner's chest, in the dark? Again, my brain searched for a reasonable answer. But to this day, I have not found one. There is no training or simulation or commonsense notion that involves shooting a firearm across the body of another person sitting twelve inches to your left.

What caused Noor to shoot in the first place? The detective reported that they had found no gun or weapon of any kind on, or near, the deceased. Now I knew that an MPD officer had shot and killed an unarmed woman for an unknown reason. Who was she and where did she come from? What brought her out into this alley in her pajamas?

At that point in my inquiry, a call came through from dispatch that unscrambled the puzzle pieces and snapped them together. Over the radio, dispatch said to us, "Squads out at the scene, we have a man who's calling in from out of town because he's concerned about his fiancée. She dialed 911 about a possible sexual assault occurring in the alley behind their house. He hasn't heard anything since. He called her back but she isn't answering."

A deeper sense of unease descended on the alley as we looked at one another and quickly confirmed with dispatch the address of the 911 caller. A patrol supervisor and a couple of officers walked around to the front of the house. They found the front door ajar, so they announced themselves and entered. The house appeared to be empty. Inside, they saw a photo of the victim. This was her house, and she was the woman who had called 911 for help.

This unthinkable tragedy set off a firestorm of outrage that reached across nine thousand miles to the doorstep of the Australian prime minister when it became known that the victim was a dual Australian American citizen. Her name was Justine Ruszczyk, but she had already begun using the last name of her fiancé, Don Damond. They were scheduled to be married in Hawaii the following month.

That night, instead of getting a call back from Justine, Don Damond received a call from me. I had to tell him the absolute worst news of his life. Later, I would sit next to Justine's father, searching for words that wouldn't come. Instead, I took out my phone, pulled up a picture of my own daughter, and set it down before him. "I have a daughter, too," I said. "And I would move heaven and earth to protect her." These were the only words that could convey the depth of sadness I felt as I apologized to Mr. Ruszczyk for the loss of his child.

It's difficult for me to grasp what entered Noor's mind and led him to conclude: "I've got to shoot and shoot now." The officers had not turned on their body-worn cameras and the squad car video did not capture the shooting, so we will never have a definitive answer. But my conclusion, then and now, is that Noor got startled by something but didn't know what he was shooting at—he just fired.

The stakes are never higher for any police officer than when they must determine whether to use force or take a life. When you fire that weapon, you can never get the bullet back. Noor didn't know what he was firing at when he discharged his weapon into the night. What he hit was an innocent woman. She wasn't armed. She wasn't a suspect. In fact, she was trying to do the right thing. She had called us for help, and we took her life.

The sun was coming up before I left the scene of the shooting. The investigation had been turned over to the Minnesota Bureau of Criminal Apprehension (BCA), as required. To ensure impartiality, the MPD had entered into an agreement with the BCA so that we did not investigate our own critical incidents of officer-involved shootings.

I briefed the mayor and left another voicemail for Chief Harteau. I made it clear: This was a bad situation. That was in the early morning hours of Saturday, and it turned out, unfortunately, that many of my initial calls and voicemail messages indicating the severity of the situation were not returned with the immediacy that I was expecting. Mayor Hodges and I held a press conference later Saturday to brief the media on the facts of the case. By Monday, Mayor Hodges had appeared on *Good Morning America* to face tough questions about the legitimacy of Noor's deadly action.

Four days after the shooting, Chief Harteau called me to say she was flying back the next day and wanted us to hold a press conference. I told her, "Chief, respectfully, there is nothing we can say that's going to make this situation better." She said, "We're going to do it anyway."

Of course, the reporters' questions were not confined to the details of the case. The media wanted to know: Where had Harteau been? Justine's parents were able to get to Minnesota from Australia days ago—why couldn't Harteau get here sooner? Instead of leveling with them, Harteau dodged. "I was out of town," was all she said. An Australian journalist then expertly set out to prove the adage that you can run, but you can't hide—especially in the age of social media. First, the reporter asked Harteau how she felt about Justine's death. Harteau expressed that she was devastated. Next, the reporter held up a printed screenshot from Harteau's Facebook page. "You said you were devastated?" she asked rhetorically as all the cameras in the room focused on a photo of Harteau taken shortly after Justine's death. It pictured Harteau with her partner on vacation in Telluride, Colorado, riding a gondola and smiling at the camera.

Now, not only had someone in uniform shot an innocent person outside her home, but also the chief, who represents the police department, appeared not to care. I've been in many press conferences that have gone off the rails, but this felt self-inflicted. I knew there would be no coming back from that.

In my view, what often accelerates a leader's downfall is a lack of humility. Humility tells us when a given circumstance is bigger than ourselves. It signals when it's time to sacrifice our wants or abandon our plans for the greater good, especially when we are a leader. Humility enables us to listen to advice and to consider an opposing point of view. It counterbalances ego-driven decisions. As several media outlets chased Harteau down to return phone calls during a calamity, to those we serve, her actions said: "I'm the chief and I will do what I want. I'm on vacation, and that's where I'm going to stay." But also: "I know this probably doesn't look great, so I'm going to try to avoid telling the whole truth about where I have been."

If you find yourself avoiding transparency, that is almost always a bad sign. At this point, the chief had lost the confidence of the mayor. The next day, the two met and Harteau texted me afterward. "I resigned," she said. "You've got the helm." Mayor Hodges called to confirm. "Rondo, you're going to be the acting chief finishing out Harteau's term."

These are the circumstances under which I became chief of the Minneapolis Police Department. On day one, I was responsible for holding an MPD officer accountable for the killing of an unarmed civilian under circumstances that called for termination and criminal charges. I testified for the prosecution in Noor's 2019 trial, which resulted in a conviction for third-degree murder and manslaughter. The first of these charges was later overturned. Noor was re-sentenced, ultimately serving more than three years in prison for manslaughter.

Following the devastating loss of his fiancée, Don Damond showed incredible grace, in keeping with Justine's generous, loving spirit and her passion for wellness. Mr. Damond partnered with me to introduce new mindfulness and wellness training for officers to support them in staying calm, collected, and compassionate.

I stepped into my new role as chief of police during a tragedy that drew criticism and scrutiny from the citizens of Minneapolis and from the other side of the world. I never dreamed that such a crisis would happen again during my tenure, but leaders do not get to pick the crises they are dealt. When a bad thing happens and the pressure's on, not every decision a leader makes will be perfect. That's okay, because as long as you continually try to do the right thing, you can adjust. The three things every leader must do in a crisis are act honestly, act decisively, and act quickly—because time is your enemy.

I don't have the answer to why it happens, but there's often a sense during a crisis that if somehow we can suspend reality, things will just work themselves out. But life doesn't work that way. There's no reset button. You've got to deal with things in real time, in real life. If you are not present when an incident occurs, you are expected to deal with it anyway. And even after you've addressed the crisis in front of you, there may be more to come. There's no pause button either. The David Campbells of the world don't just vanish; the gunfire doesn't simply cease. When the unexpected, or even the unthinkable, occurs, it's critical to have a clear, concise set of guiding principles in place so that you don't become disoriented or overwhelmed.

And so, one of the first things I did when I became chief was to sit down at my little two-seat kitchen table with a notepad to write down my vision for the Minneapolis Police Department. The MPD policy and procedure manual is well over five hundred pages. There is no conceivable way that even the smartest person could learn every word by heart. My goal was to define our North Star, clearly and memorably. I wrote out a three-page statement that I emailed to all sworn and civilian staff.

I let everyone know: When you find yourself in a challenging situation, or when there's a gray or murky area, just go back to this vision statement. If you do that, we'll be all right. I was not asking anyone to be perfect. I told everyone who worked for me: If you make a good faith mistake while you adhere to this path, I've got your back. I will support you and we'll take the lumps. Ultimately, I am responsible.

The principles that must guide our actions are simple. Sanctity of life is the most precious of all your duties. Rely on communication and de-escalation. Minimize harm and the risk of harm. Do not be baited by disrespect to respond in kind. We must serve all our communities without bias or favor. Discrimination of any kind has absolutely no place or refuge in the MPD. Be truthful in all you say or put in writing. Untruths are unacceptable. Silence is complicity. Hold each other accountable. You or your colleague may be going through something, so seek the resources now that the department offers. But don't do the bad thing and then say: "Oh, I need help." If an employee has tarnished the badge by doing something egregious, they will not be given a pass because they're struggling.

The majority of individuals in the MPD had never met me. They would be receiving directives, policies, and emails from someone they didn't know. I wanted to let them know what mattered to me, and what they could expect of me. The values expressed in my vision statement are rooted in procedural justice. In its simplest form, procedural justice is a way for us to understand one another. It doesn't require a budget or an advanced degree. It simply says that we will give others a voice. We will treat others with dignity and respect. Our engagement will be neutral. This means I'm not going to pre-judge you. If there is one opportunity for trust to develop, we're going to seize it. That's all it is. It works best when we can meet each other halfway. But even if a community member walks away unsatisfied, they are not likely to conclude that the undesired outcome was the result of bias. We just didn't agree—and that's okay.

As one of the five officers who filed the discrimination lawsuit in 2007, I was well aware that it would be challenging to make improvements to a broken system. A big swing in culture has to be cumulative over time. The old ways persist because culture is stubborn and people typically resist change. So one effective way to create change is to bring new people with new ideas into the culture. New hires are like saplings that will take many years to grow. You may never see their potential come to fruition. But it's a great place to start. I notified human resources that we were going to do things differently.

The 2007 lawsuit had taught me that policy changes can make a difference, so in 2017 I made swift changes to MPD hiring practices. Individually, these changes may seem small—but I believed collectively they would have a significant impact. I interviewed every candidate before a hire was approved. I didn't delegate interviews to supervisors because when bad hires happen, the community's not going to ask, "Who is the supervising lieutenant that hired this person?" They're going to look to the chief. The number one quality I sought in a candidate was character. I'd rather make due with one less officer than hire someone without character. It's not worth it. I had an obligation to the people of Minneapolis—my 430,000 bosses—to make sure all employees had the right mindset to do the job.

That mindset was evaluated, in large part, by a pre-employment psychologist who met with candidates for a series of interviews. The psychologist was a critical gatekeeper, and it was time for a new hire to fill this role. I wrote a position description that required candidates to be competent in procedural justice and to have a thorough understanding of implicit bias. The new psychologist was going to evaluate candidates for their ability to uphold my vision statement. I sat in on the job interview for Jan Tyson Roberts, PhD, who not only met these criteria but also had a deep understanding of the city and its communities. I hired her as the first African American woman in that position in the history of the department. She is still with the organization—just one example of how good hires can create a legacy that lasts far longer than any individual leader.

With the right person in place as the pre-employment psychologist, I began to reform our hiring policies. It was my view that the city had been using some blunt tools for the delicate job of hiring peace officers. For decades, human resources and hiring managers had placed a lot of weight on a candidate's credit history. One's credit history can, perhaps, show a lack of financial responsibility. But the credit score alone doesn't take into account the individual and their journey. If a single mom is working two jobs and going to school when she falls behind on bills because her rent was raised or her child got sick, should she be excluded from consideration? I made sure that human resources understood the reasons behind any credit issues that came up, and that they would take them into account.

Another oversimplified aspect of background checks for employment was how many 911 calls were placed to a candidate's address. This, too, cannot be taken at face value. For example, I interviewed one candidate from the East Coast who had the character to wear the badge. But at the end of our conversation he said, "Chief, I want to share something with you if I can. In the past I have gotten to a certain point in the hiring process and I'm denied. They see that back East there have been several 911 calls to my residence. But what they didn't know is that I live with my mother and I have an older brother who was involved in some bad things. Every call was because of him." We looked into this, and verified that it was true. I wanted everyone involved in the hiring process to think about who gets passed over and why—because we are not going to change the culture if we don't look closely at who we admit to the profession, and who we exclude.

On my first day as chief, I received a letter that would, again, reaffirm my commitment to public service—this time through the gift of unexpected solidarity. I walked into my new office to find an envelope on my desk. I could tell immediately from its bold markings that it came from the Minnesota Department of Corrections. It was from Kevin Walker, a former teammate I had played football with in high school. Kevin fell into substance abuse during the crack cocaine era. As a young man, he was arrested, charged, and convicted for murder. For all of his adult life, he had been incarcerated in Minnesota prisons.

The letter began, "Rondo, I've been thinking about you and praying for you. I wanted to let you know I'm working with a young men's restorative justice group in prison so when they go back into the community they will have a chance to make it. Can you come here and talk to them?" I was so touched that he had reached out to me through the department of prisons. Of course I said yes.

The separation between me and Kevin is thin and fragile. During our youth we were equally aware of the temptations that lead to wrong choices and, at times, tragic consequences for some in our community. Perhaps I had just one more positive adult in my life who gave me a bit more tough love. Maybe when I was confronted with similar choices as Kevin, I had just a few more seconds than he did to make the better choice. We grew up in the same neighborhood, went to the same school, played on the same sports team, and hung out at some of the same parties. All I know is that one day Kevin made a choice that resulted in a life taken and required him to pay his debt to society. While doing so, he had made another choice: to try his best to influence young men in prison to lead productive lives and set a positive example for their children if they return to our community. I commend him for that.

When I entered the prison at Faribault, wearing my uniform, I had some apprehension about how I would be received. It's a surreal experience when those big prison doors slam shut behind you. It affects your psyche. There's an instant awareness that your ability to move about freely is gone, even if you're the chief of police for a major city just fifty miles away. I had no gun and no rank there. Make no bones about it, when I entered the prison, I was vulnerable like everyone else.

When I saw Kevin, we hugged. It was an emotional embrace, resonant with memories of our days on the football team. Kevin was a large, strong young man in high school. He was a defensive lineman while I was a running back. Although a vast gulf separates our circumstances today, we are both doing what we can to help others. Kevin is helping younger men to understand that their mistakes don't have to define them. Based on Kevin's letter, I had come prepared to speak with a group of around a dozen men. I was surprised to discover that Kevin had aimed for much higher attendance. I found myself looking out at an audience of 150. Kevin apologized for what he considered a low turnout, making sure to let me know that in the afternoon session there would be 200.

I quickly adjusted my expectations and began to speak. The most valued currency in prison is respect, so I did not stand before these men to deliver any BS. Incarcerated individuals can detect BS immediately. Once they do, you lose all credibility and you will have broken the golden rule by disrespecting them. I knew that no matter how large or small the audience was, they would accept nothing less than an honest, open conversation.

Right away I noticed a man with tattoos on his neck, pacing back and forth at the back of the room, glaring at me with piercing eyes. I could tell he wasn't happy. I went ahead with my talk, all the while keeping an eye on him. When the question-and-answer session began, he stood in a long line to speak to me. "Chief Rondo," he said into the microphone, "when I first heard that you were coming here, I was pissed. I was angry. I felt that your people are the reason I'm in here." He stopped speaking for a moment and began to cry. "Then I heard you say that while we're in here doing our time, you and your officers are looking out for our kids and protecting them when we can't be there. I have kids at Little Earth and I worry about them."

As a father myself, I felt this man and I shared an immediate understanding. Our children are front and center in our minds and hearts. I walked up to the man and gave him a hug. I understood the environment of Little Earth, an urban subsidized housing complex for Native American residents near the neighborhood where I grew up. As chief, I knew something about the challenges the residents face. This man can't reach out to hug and protect his kids, so he was relying on me to live up to my oath to take care of the kids in our community. He understood that the oath doesn't say I have to know you or have gone to school with you to look out for your kids. His willingness to listen, and to place his trust in me, affected me deeply. He was saying: I need you to look after my babies because I can't. I wasn't going to let him down.

8
Leading While Black

PEOPLE OFTEN ASK ME HOW IT FEELS TO BE THE FIRST BLACK CHIEF OF POLICE in the history of the Minneapolis Police Department. I understand the question, but I'm not sure how to answer it. The subtext to this well-meaning query seems to be, "Can you believe it?" Well, yes. I didn't wake up the morning of my swearing-in ceremony as chief and suddenly realize, "I'm Black!" I was chief by choice and Black by birth. I was Black when I received hate mail in 1992. I was Black when I joined the discrimination lawsuit against the department in 2007. I was Black when I was appointed Commander of the Internal Affairs Unit and Inspector of the 1st Precinct. How does it feel to be the first Black chief of police in my city? It's complicated. For one thing, I can't take full credit for my appointment to the office. A great web of ancestors, community members, and civic leaders made it possible.

The Minneapolis Police Department was created four years after the Emancipation Proclamation. The seeds of its culture were planted a century before I was born. There are elders in Minneapolis who thought they'd never live to see the day when a Black person would become chief of police. For them, this milestone came sooner than they had dared to hope. From the elders' vantage point, they could look back and recall the multitude of smaller steps that had cumulatively led to big changes. On the other hand, some in the community wanted transformational change in the MPD and they wanted it seemingly overnight. The young people, especially, had decided that enough was enough and they would evaluate me by my ability to deliver swift, sweeping changes. Having worked for change from within this system for decades, I understood both perspectives.

The way I see it, my five and a half years in office formed one link in a chain forged by fifty-two Minneapolis police chiefs before me. I knew what kind of department I wanted to hand over to the fifty-fourth chief. As chief number fifty-three, my North Star was to build a department that would uphold the ideals of procedural justice in every interaction a police officer had with a civilian. This work would have to be done without a playbook, in the midst of multiple crises, and during a time when our city was facing not only a deficit of hope but also a deficit of trust.

When Minneapolis descended into chaos following the indefensible, inhumane actions of a white police officer who murdered a Black citizen, it was my responsibility as the police chief to bring peace to the city. As the city's first *Black* police chief, it was my calling to define "peace" according to the words of Dr. Martin Luther King Jr.: "True peace is not merely the absence of tension; it is the presence of justice."

I hope no other city has to go through the trauma that Minneapolis faced in 2020. But if that happens, I believe Minneapolis will stand as a model for how we can get through tough times if we put aside our grievances and come together for the common good. At the same time, the events in Minneapolis serve as a warning to changemakers that we must be aware of the forces that want us to fail. Those forces may come from outside the organization, from the darker regions of our society. Those forces may come from within the organization. Bad culture is like quicksand; just when you think you're able to wriggle free, it wraps around you and pulls you in deeper.

We will never evolve in the policing profession if we do not address race head-on. Race is inextricably a part of the American policing system, all the way back to the Civil War and Reconstruction, through the Jim Crow era, to the Civil Rights Movement, to the summer of 2020 and beyond. The end of slavery was a seismic shift in our nation. For the first time, at least in principle, it was acknowledged that slavery was a sin and a stain on America. For more than two hundred years, we deprived a swath of our American population—Black Americans—of their human rights and denied them civil rights. More soldiers lost their lives in the Civil War than in the two World Wars combined. There was a great deal of support for the ideological belief that slavery was wrong. Nevertheless, the abolition of slavery was a major shock to the American system. As it so often does, fear accompanied this change. The old beliefs did not simply vanish with General Robert E. Lee's surrender. In the post–Civil War era, local police departments and sheriffs played a significant role in either holding onto the debilitating norms of racism, or in trying to protect the newly won rights of Black Americans. That was the divide within American law enforcement from the beginning, and its legacy persists to this day.

In some parts of our country, after the Civil War, sheriffs and police officers were stationed outside polling places to intimidate voters, rubbing the butts of their guns when Black men and women came to cast a ballot. In the 1920s, NAACP chapters campaigned so that law enforcement would not ignore the scourge of lynchings or sweep it aside. Some police officers and sheriffs were active members of organized hate groups like the KKK. During the civil rights era, some of the most shocking—and galvanizing—images from the marches in the South showed police officers beating Black men, pulling Black women by their hair or blouses, and deploying attack dogs and fire hoses on the civil rights marchers. This recent history was passed down to me by elders who witnessed or experienced it firsthand. History is not a dusty relic; it's personal. While I am too young to have been bitten by a dog sicced on me by Bull Connor, I am old enough to feel the menace when a colleague, cloaked in anonymity, invokes the KKK in a letter addressed to me in 1992.

Even though Minnesota is a northern state, it is not beyond the reach of racial violence or atrocities in which the police were complicit. The picturesque town of Duluth, 150 miles north of Minneapolis along the shore of Lake Superior, was the site of one of the ugliest moments in the state's history. In June 1920, a white woman falsely accused a group of young Black men of rape. The men were workers for a traveling circus, just passing through town. Police arrested six men and held them in the Duluth City Jail. Newspaper coverage of the arrests roiled the town. Soon, as many as ten thousand angry white people thronged the streets outside the jail.

When it became clear that the mob's intention was to storm the jail, the Duluth police officers kept their weapons holstered. They didn't fire a single warning shot to try to push back the crowd. This order came from Duluth's commissioner of public safety, who had said, "I don't want a single drop of white blood shed for these n——s." The police were responsible for the men in their custody. This tenet is as old as policing itself: in our custody, in our care. The men had not been tried, much less convicted, for the crime they were accused of. A few officers, in defiance of the commissioner's stance, went out into the street and tried to fight off the mob with a fire hose. But those officers who did not even try, and the commissioner who deemed the Black men unworthy of his protection, were complicit in the fate of the prisoners.

The crowd overran the jail and began to break through the bars on the cells. They got hold of Isaac McGhie and carried him into the street, beating him as they dragged him one block uphill to a lamppost. McGhie was the first to be hanged. The proprietor of a nearby hardware store gave the mob the rope, and said it was on the house. A local priest tried to stop the enraged crowd, climbing partway up the lamppost himself and begging the crowd to show mercy. They pulled the priest down and went on with the execution. Next the mob snatched Elias Clayton and Elmer Jackson from their cell, beat them, stripped them to the waist, and lynched them from the same lamppost. After the carnage, members of the crowd posed for photographs with the lifeless bodies. These gruesome images were later reproduced on commemorative postcards, available for sale to tourists.

Any person who wears a uniform and badge in any police department in this country should know the history of this profession. My uncle Darren was certainly aware of it in 1992 when he refused to get into a squad car, by himself, with the white officer who had just called him the N-word. We don't have to reach back to our great-grandparents' era to find incidents of police killings of Black people that sparked outrage. In our own lifetimes, many incidents have affirmed the deep-rooted distrust that some Black people in our country have toward the policing profession—whether or not an officer's use of deadly force was deemed justified by the courts. George Floyd was preceded by Eric Garner, Breonna Taylor, Freddie Gray, Tamir Rice, Michael Brown, and others, nationally.

His death was preceded by Philando Castile, Jamar Clark, and others, in Minnesota. Not only did Derek Chauvin crush George Floyd under his knee for more than nine minutes, three other officers at the scene failed to stop him.

It's also true that there are examples of police officers who protected Black students during school desegregation nationally or, in Minneapolis, protected Arthur and Edith Lee from a white mob just eleven years after the lynchings in Duluth and some thirty years before the beginning of the Civil Rights Movement. History is layered and multifaceted. It does not always supply easy answers, but it is imperative that we learn from it. As a nation, we must be willing to have difficult conversations about the dynamics of race and policing.

In Black families, these difficult conversations take place between parents and their children in a rite of passage so ubiquitous it is known simply as "the talk." This refers to the instruction Black parents must give to our children about how to behave so that they can survive an encounter with the wrong police officer on the wrong day. When I take off my uniform, I am treated the same as any other Black man in America. I had to give my son the talk just like other Black fathers. In many Black households, parents deliver the talk when their teenager gets a driver's license.

My days as the family chauffeur were coming to an end. I felt both excitement and dread for my son, Medaria, to take on the responsibility of driving. While it was absolutely a requirement that I teach him how to change lanes and parallel park—as every parent must—there was an added mandate for me as a Black father. Medaria was about to be driving independently in the city, out of my reach and no longer in my care.

As a young Black male, my son is disproportionately likely to be pulled over by the police. I needed him to understand that his engagement with a police officer is governed by an inherent power imbalance, from the minute he rolls down the driver's-side window. His survival can depend on his acceptance and understanding of this dynamic. Yes, my son is a citizen and yes, he has civil rights and freedom of speech. But here's the caveat: He doesn't have the right to detain someone or use deadly force if justified. Period. Full stop. Only the police officer has those rights. If my son sees red lights flashing behind him, I need him to understand that this imbalance exists with the most professional police officers—and with the least professional police officers. Police departments across the country are imperfect, because society is imperfect, and that's where police departments get their officers from.

The talk teaches our Black children that showing respect is the best way to fortify themselves during an encounter with the police. I have raised my children to be universally respectful. That's how I was raised, too. But now, at sixteen, my son would have to learn that the respectfulness taught down through the generations is not, and has never been, solely a matter of manners. Respect has a more important significance during a police encounter, because it could save his life. Yes, the police officer should also be respectful—but even if he or she isn't, my son has to be. That's nonnegotiable. Even if it means his pride is hurt. I'm well aware that the invisible scars of wounded dignity are the most difficult to heal and have been inflicted on generation after generation of Black people. But we can work on healing those wounds together if my son comes home. If he feels his rights have been violated, we can file a complaint—but only if he lives to fight another day.

"The talk" includes specific instructions on what to do and say: "Yes, Officer. No, Officer. Here, Officer, my driver's license and insurance card are in the glove compartment. Would you like me to get them for you?" Keep your hands on the steering wheel during this conversation. Don't make any furtive movements. Make eye contact. You should neither confront the officer nor flee—because if you do, your odds of walking away from this encounter will plummet. You must instead try to tip the odds in your favor because you don't have the advantage. This encounter is not equal. It was never intended to be.

The stakes of this lesson are life or death, but parents are speaking to kids who have only been on the earth for sixteen years. Black parents must have this talk with our teenagers whether they have the emotional maturity for it or not. After spending sixteen years working to instill confidence and self-assurance in our children, we as parents now have to make sure they can integrate this new message. Yes, we've been teaching you about your own worth and power—but if you find yourself in an encounter with the police, all that needs to go in the back seat because your safety depends on it. The talk is like the passenger safety instruction required by the Federal Aviation Administration. Most planes are going to take off and land just fine. A water landing is unlikely. But they're telling you about the flotation device for a reason—because that kind of disaster has happened before.

As I said, being a Black police chief is complicated. I existed in two worlds—one I came from and one I worked hard to join. At times, those worlds were in conflict. But when they were in harmony, my profession enabled me to serve the people of Minneapolis and keep them safe. In those moments of harmony, I could glimpse a world that might be, a future world in which the Minneapolis Police Department earned, and was worthy of, the public trust. Perhaps in this world, my son wouldn't need to give his son "the talk." If police officers perform their jobs in a procedurally just way, a teenaged driver who is pulled over will still need to understand and respect the inherent imbalance between us. But he won't need to fear its repercussions every time he borrows the car keys, because officers will have risen above any temptation to flex that power or to use it to intimidate. When police officers give voice, show respect, are neutral, and build spaces of trust, a brighter future is possible. And in this brighter future, the officer won't have pulled the driver over just because he is Black. There are many policies in place now to move us closer to that world, including body-worn cameras and measures to prevent biased traffic stops. But there is more work to be done. We've got to do all we can as a society to prevent any new entries in the ledger of police violence and intimidation. History is important, and we will never clear the shelf. But we shouldn't be adding any more books to it.

When Minneapolis mayor Betsy Hodges appointed me chief of police in 2017, I wanted to bridge and honor my two worlds from the minute I put on the chief's insignia. To my knowledge, my swearing-in ceremony was the first ever to be held in the community, rather than at City Hall. At my request, it took place at Sabathani Community Center, one of Minnesota's oldest African American-founded nonprofit service organizations. Sabathani is in the heart of South Minneapolis, where I grew up. I used to browse the stacks of vinyl at Crown Records down the street, and would gather my loose change to buy snacks at Mr. Ruben's Black-owned grocery store nearby. Sabathani Community Center is filled with good memories, and it was the perfect place to celebrate a career milestone. My swearing-in ceremony was not just a rite of passage for me, but it was also an acknowledgment of those who came before me and who had dreamed of a day like this. I was surrounded by neighbors, family, and friends who had known me since I had attended dances in that very building as a teenager. If it's possible to be humbled and proud at the same time, that is how I felt looking out at the room filled with people representing the great diversity of our city, including leaders of Native and Indigenous, Latino, African, Asian, and LGBTQ+ communities, as well as faith leaders. Dr. Josie Johnson, a Minnesota civil rights icon, spoke from the podium that day. Born in 1930, Dr. Johnson had led the Minnesota delegation to Dr. King's March on Washington in 1963 and had traveled to Mississippi the following year during the Freedom Summer. She was one of the leaders who helped the North Side recover from the Plymouth Avenue riots of 1967. A renowned educator and scholar, she became the first Black regent of the University of Minnesota in 1971. Dr. Johnson was a pioneer, and she described me as a pioneer, too. The appointment of the city's first Black chief of police, she said, was a symbol of hope, representing "the promise to our children that the struggle before us all will yield this kind of result."

The struggle had brought me to a corner office in City Hall with panoramic views of downtown Minneapolis. It came with an assigned parking space, a marker of status as deluxe as the "scrambled eggs" now embroidered on the brim of my hat, in swirls of golden thread. In my new spacious office, above my desk, I hung a photograph to honor the long lineage of Black officers in the MPD.

The photograph is a portrait taken sometime in the 1890s. It shows about twenty officers from the Minneapolis Police Department's 1st Precinct, assembled in neat rows and dressed in uniforms similar to the old "Bobby" style of English police officers. Some of the men have big handlebar mustaches. What stands out is one officer seated at the far left. He is Henry G. Thompson, the only African American officer in the portrait. He was probably in his early thirties at the time the photograph was taken. He was married and had four small children.

As a Minneapolis police officer, Thompson was assigned to a horse-drawn wagon that patrolled the milling district along the banks of the Mississippi River. One of his functions was to pick up drunks outside the pubs where men got rowdy after their shifts in the mills. During that time, there were very few Black officers in the city and they were not allowed to arrest white people. Thompson could only drive the wagon. When the white officers arrested the drunk and disorderly, they were loaded into Thompson's wagon— known as the Black Mariah—and he took them to the hoosegow.

When I look at Thompson's portrait, I can see pain and pride. I can see in his facial expression and in the immaculate state of his uniform that he represented a purpose greater than just himself. He would have watched stonemasons setting the granite slabs that built the City Hall where I had hung his photo. He wouldn't live to see it, but perhaps he dreamed that, someday, someone who looked like him would be sitting at the chief's desk inside that grand building.

There is a connective thread that links us to the spirit of our ancestors—and often it is pain, suffering, and the fight for survival that connects us. When I would swivel my chair around at my desk and look up at Henry G. Thompson's face, it grounded me. I saw an officer who worked seventy-five years before the Civil Rights Act, who wasn't even allowed to arrest white people, and I knew that my hardest days did not come close to his. And yet, whatever discrimination he experienced, he never quit. He served out a full career. On my hardest days, I could imagine him whispering to me from generations long ago, "Okay, Rondo, so what are you going to do now? You can't quit. You've got to fight. Whatever challenge you're facing, they're watching how you respond."

I was fully aware of the shoulders I was standing on to attain the role of chief. I understood that being a "first," or an "only," comes with its own set of pressures and expectations. I would be scrutinized from the shine on my shoes to the grammar in my memos. That's just the way it is. Being the first didn't lessen my load. If anything, I had a more immense responsibility. But I was okay with that. When put into perspective, taking on this increased burden was my way of giving back to my predecessors for never letting their vision die. I took comfort in knowing that, hopefully, the next Black chief could purely be judged on his or her merit. But make no mistake, for any "first," the magnifying glass will be much sharper and the scrutiny much more intense. Even when I was making a decision based on matters that had absolutely nothing to do with race, inevitably there would be those who insisted on viewing my actions through that lens. I decided that the best way to live up to the expectations placed on me was to stay focused, stay principled, and stay true to myself.

Like any achievement, my appointment as chief of police came at a cost. For more than twenty-five years, I had sacrificed time with my family to the demands of my career. Time is the most valuable currency that anyone has on this earth. There's no refund on time spent. You can never replace it or get it back. When I missed my daughter's singing performances or my son's football games, I gave up time that was meant to be shared as a family. My children are missing some memories of their father clapping loudly in the auditorium or cheering from the bleachers. My family made adjustments. Early in my career when I was asked to attend a birthday party or a barbecue, I'd reply, "Oh, absolutely, that's four months out; I'll be there!" Eventually, wishful thinking gave way to a more respectful realism, and I'd say truthfully, "I'll do my best. I'll be there if I can." My siblings and parents and aunts and uncles knew what this meant. "Rondo probably won't be there. If he shows up, we'll be thrilled. But we don't have to prepare an extra table setting for Rondo."

While these lost moments accumulated over time, leaving blank spots in the family photos where my face should have been, I was working late nights and sleeping in my office at City Hall, keeping

my toiletry bag stocked and stashing a few clean and pressed uniforms at work. As I advanced in my career, being "off duty" still
meant having to carry two cell phones at all times. It didn't guarantee I'd make it to the apple pie dessert course at Thanksgiving
dinner. Even if I had a moment when I could get to a grocery store
on the weekend, I knew I'd be cutting my shopping list short if the
phone rang from the precinct or from City Hall.

My children came along with me on this journey, but they didn't
sign up for it. I know what that cost me, but I only have some idea
what it cost my son and daughter, who were young adults on the
day I was sworn in as chief. The unconditional love and support
of my children on that day, and in all the years preceding it, meant
more to me than the new badge my daughter pinned to my chest as
I raised my right hand to take the oath as the city's first Black chief.

9

Unconventional Allies

IN 2015 I BECAME AWARE OF A POWERFUL VOICE ADVOCATING FOR RACIAL JUSTICE and police reform in the Twin Cities. Nekima Levy Armstrong had come to Minnesota by way of Jackson, Mississippi, where she was born, and South Los Angeles, where she grew up. She was a professor of law at the University of St. Thomas Law School, where she founded and directed a civil rights legal clinic. She also served as president of the Minneapolis NAACP. Suddenly, Nekima Levy Armstrong seemed to be everywhere, on television and in radio interviews, speaking with great passion about the issues that also preoccupied me. I heard the fire in her voice when she discussed the reasons behind the distrust that some in the Black community felt toward the MPD.

I was a deputy chief of staff at the time, and Armstrong was someone I wanted to meet. So I called her up and she agreed to meet with me in her office on the university campus. We truly connected when Armstrong said to me, "Rondo, I am the mother of two Black sons and I don't want my boys to be shot by the police."

When she spoke to me as a mother, I responded as a father. I told her that I, too, have a son. I would do anything to protect him, and I will do everything I can to protect her sons, too.

Armstrong showed me that she wanted real change and racial justice, particularly for our children. These were the early days of the Black Lives Matter movement and Nekima Levy Armstrong was part of a new wave of activism. The previous year she had traveled to Ferguson, Missouri, to protest the police killing of Michael Brown, an unarmed Black teenager. Armstrong made it clear that we needed police accountability in Minneapolis. Community members were willing to work with the police department, she said, but they needed to be heard. The people shouldn't have to take to the streets to draw attention to issues that we already know are a problem, she said. The department must do the work, and performative measures will not be acceptable. I left our first meeting feeling that I had made a real connection that we could build on. I thought, if I show Nekima Levy Armstrong I'm genuine, we will continue to talk.

A few months later, on November 15, 2015, I received a text shortly after midnight, alerting me that a young Black man had been shot and killed by an MPD officer responding to a domestic disturbance call. I was deputy chief at the time. I knew this was a major incident, and I wanted to inform Armstrong immediately, and personally. I called her before I left the house. "I don't have all the details," I told her, "but I'm heading to the scene now and I will keep you updated."

Outside an apartment building on Plymouth Avenue in North Minneapolis, MPD officers Mark Ringgenberg and Dustin Schwarze, both white, had attempted to arrest twenty-four-year-old Jamar Clark. His girlfriend was being treated by paramedics at the scene, and Clark had been accused of assaulting her. The officers later testified that they were attempting to handcuff Clark when he grabbed Ringgenberg's holstered gun, prompting Schwarze to shoot Clark in self-defense. Some witnesses, however, said that Clark was already handcuffed when he was shot. These conflicting accounts aroused suspicion and left community members with unanswered questions. Unfortunately, given its track record, the MPD had not earned the benefit of the doubt.

Armstrong and others felt it was necessary to apply immediate pressure for the MPD and outside investigators to account for the officers' actions. Armstrong arrived on the scene shortly after I did, and knocked on doors to locate witnesses. She called an impromptu press conference to point out the discrepancies in the accounts of Clark's death, and she demanded transparency from the MPD. The response from young activists was swift as Armstrong and others issued a call-to-action. Dozens of protesters gathered within about ninety minutes to march from the scene of the shooting to the nearby 4th Precinct. The protesters demanded the release of the officers' names and the release of the dashcam video. At the time, body-worn cameras were just being introduced in the MPD and were not yet in use in the 4th Precinct. The primary video evidence would come from a camera on the ambulance at the scene—but as the Bureau of Criminal Apprehension conducted its investigation, they found that this camera did not capture the shooting.

Hundreds gathered outside the 4th Precinct, chanting and carrying homemade banners. Their numbers were large enough to shut down Plymouth Avenue North and surround the precinct building. Protesters occupied the entry vestibule and blocked the doors. I was witnessing a seismic shift from the days when groups that wanted to have demonstrations went down to City Hall and filled out a permit that included the date and time of the protest, the size of the crowd they expected, and the route they planned to march. Now, using social media, activists could assemble massive crowds in a very short time—and events could be staged at multiple locations simultaneously. That November in 2015, I was witnessing the coalescing of a movement that had begun the year before in Ferguson. Young people were paying attention, organizing, and willing to fight for justice.

The movement came to my front door when hundreds of mostly young people seated themselves on the streets and sidewalks outside the 4th Precinct, bundled in warm coats and undeterred by the cold November temperatures. I was still in the mindset that while these young people had a point to make, the precinct officers also had work to do. Surely there could be mutual accommodation. All I needed was for the protesters to clear a pathway to the precinct parking lot gate so the officers could go in and out. I noticed a Black man about twenty years old, wearing a dark jacket, jeans, and a beanie hat, calmly giving instructions to the protesters seated around him. Even the older people were giving him their attention, so it seemed he had some influence. The Black Lives Matter group didn't seem to have a designated leader or spokesperson to negotiate with, so I decided to approach the young man. To this day, I cringe as I recall what happened next. Dressed in my winter uniform with a leather jacket and hat, I slowly picked my way through the densely packed crowd, trying to avoid stepping on the people sitting cross-legged in my path. When I reached the man I said, "Hello, excuse me, but you're blocking the entrance to the precinct parking lot. I'd really appreciate it if I could get half of you to move over this way, and the rest of you to move the other way—because we've got calls to go on." I punctuated this request with a gesture, miming the parting of the crowd. A hush fell as dozens of faces swiveled toward me bearing baffled expressions as if to say, "Are we getting punked? Is this guy a doofus, or what?"

Calmly, the young man began to speak. I crouched down, like a parent bending toward a small child, so I could hear him. "Are you serious?" he said. He knew I was serious and yet he could hardly believe that I had failed to grasp the situation I was in. "Yeah!" I replied politely. "If you all could just move over a bit, that would be great!" Out of the corner of my eye, I could see cell phone cameras emerging from coat pockets. The man spoke to me again in a way that was not incendiary, but educational—albeit in a remedial tone. "We aren't moving," he explained. "And you don't get to dictate our tactics according to what makes you feel comfortable."

I had been called out—and now I would have to make the excruciatingly slow and awkward tiptoe back through the crowd. "Rondo," I thought, "welcome to the world of discomfort!" The man's statement was powerful and he was right. The very nature of protests is meant to make systems uncomfortable. The activism I expected and understood was rooted in Dr. King's peaceful civil disobedience, but I was standing there in 2015, not 1965. When I finally caught on, I understood that there was a new chapter being created by a new generation. I was not the author. I was a player in their book—and I'm going to be known as The Doofus—but I was not writing the book; they were. This was not a throwback to the sit-ins of old. This was an occupation.

For the next eighteen days, protesters occupied a police precinct in a major US city—a situation that, to my knowledge, was unprecedented. One day, after walking into the encampment to speak to the group, I returned to my car to find my tires slashed. In time, the standoff erupted into hours-long, violent clashes as some in the crowd threw bricks and lobbed Molotov cocktails over the chain-link fence, and officers sprayed the crowd with chemical irritants. The video footage of these skirmishes is nearly indistinguishable from scenes that would occur five years later outside the 3rd Precinct across town.

Aside from the small group that occupied the vestibule, protesters slept outside with only tents to shield them from the snow. Scattered fires provided warmth but enveloped the camp in a haze of smoke, raising concerns about safety. Piles of garbage accumulated among the tents. Still, the protesters' needs for food, water, and other supplies were met by their supporters, enabling them to hold out despite the miserable conditions. Meanwhile, officers continued their work from spare desks in neighboring precincts and in squad cars deployed from a temporary base camp in a nearby parking lot.

As the days went by, this protracted engagement was predictably beset by emotional and physical fatigue on both sides. That's why it's crucial to seek actionable understanding within the first forty-eight hours of a conflict or demonstration. If it goes on much longer, both sides hunker down and a sense of frustration takes over. Each side believes the other is not listening and, in return, will become determined not to back down. At that point, it becomes a game of attrition. In the beginning, however, there may be a clear focal point for the protest and enough goodwill to open a dialogue on how the situation can be resolved. By day six, or day ten, or day fourteen that initial goodwill fades and becomes secondary to a test of wills. Meanwhile, the media that served to bring attention to the cause or conflict has moved on.

The longer the occupation went on, the less the general public understood what the message was. Neighborhood residents were watching the trash accumulate, breathing in smoke, and hearing noise from the encampment day and night. City buses couldn't get through the barricaded street to transport people to work and school. The fire department had checked out the encampment and determined that it was starting to become a health and public safety hazard. At some point in time, the mayor and the chief determined the disruption was unsustainable. On the eighteenth day, after notifying the protesters, the city sent in public works trucks and police officers to disband the encampment.

Even without any resolution of the issues that prompted the protest in the first place, each side could claim a victory. The protesters had reached a milestone. They had lasted for eighteen days—longer than they ever had before—and they might have gone on even longer. The police officers, on the other hand, had managed to continue their work despite the disruption. Aside from the entryway vestibule, the occupiers remained outdoors on the streets and sidewalks. From the officers' point of view, the protesters never took over the precinct. Each side could claim some kind of victory, but the underlying wounds weren't treated and the mutual distrust had not diminished.

Four months later, Hennepin County Attorney Mike Freeman announced that officers Ringgenberg and Schwarze would not face charges, and that forensic evidence did not support allegations that Clark was handcuffed when he was shot. On June 1, 2016, Federal officials also declined to prosecute the officers after an independent investigation found insufficient evidence to support criminal civil rights charges.

The encounter with police that cost Jamar Clark his life had lasted just sixty-one seconds. But its repercussions would echo through the years to ring forth again in the summer of 2020. The community doesn't forget. The MPD believed that resolution was achieved by disbanding the encampment. There was no series of meetings involving the mayor, the chief, Nekima Levy Armstrong, and other young leaders to seek an understanding of what prompted those eighteen days of protest and to determine what might prevent this from happening again.

It wasn't sixty-year-olds taking to the streets and surrounding the precinct. The times had changed, and this happens with every generation. Nevertheless, we can become attached to what's familiar and this can lead to one of the biggest mistakes that leaders make—dismissing the power and influence of those who don't conform to what you expect or what you want to believe. We can learn from young people, but too often the department did not make the effort. Instead, when there were challenges in understanding the needs or frustrations of young people, we would try to enlist community elders to go handle the talk with the youth and get them to see things our way. But the rising power of young voices in the city was about to change who we looked upon as being leaders. I knew I needed to reach out across the generations. The young people were trying to tell us that change was necessary, and they planned to hold us accountable—even if it made us uncomfortable.

10
Slow Motion Murder

ON MEMORIAL DAY IN 2020, I WAS ALONE IN AN EMPTY CITY HALL, REVIEWING NOTES
for my weekly State of the City public safety meeting. The next
morning, I would brief the mayor—noting that our city, like
others around the country, was dealing with a spike in violent
crime. The increase in shootings and carjackings was very concerning to me.

May 25 was a holiday, and it was nearly midnight. I sat at my
desk and occasionally glanced out my office windows onto the
empty Fifth Street light rail platform. Across downtown, the streets
were dark and quiet. The buses had stopped running hours ago.
No smokers huddled on the sidewalk outside the Depot Bar. No
thumping bass could be heard outside the legendary First Avenue
nightclub. The stage had gone dark when live concerts became
risky, everyone in the crowd a potential vector of a new disease.
The office buildings had been unoccupied for weeks and many of
the shops had shuttered.

Across the city, coals from Memorial Day barbecues had gone cold. While many of its 430,000 residents slept, police officers in Minneapolis were four hours into the ten-hour night shift. Patrol officers were answering calls: shots fired, domestic assault, and the usual disturbances related to the many homeless camps scattered throughout the city.

The pandemic dusted our lives with fear. For the first time, I was trying to lead a police department from a public health lens as well, ensuring officers had enough N95 masks. Many in the MPD were strictly observant of CDC guidelines. At the same time, rumors penetrated the precinct walls that COVID-19 was a hoax and a conspiracy.

At precinct roll calls, sergeants served as priests and politicians. As priests, they advised the tired officers sitting before them to have faith that, as far as the pandemic goes, "this, too, shall pass." But the lockdown had dragged on for several weeks and nobody knew when it would end. The best the sergeants could do was offer a blessing: "Make sure you and your partners stay safe out there."

As politicians, sergeants fell back on well-worn talking points when their overwhelmed staff members asked when more officers would join the ranks. "The chief's administration and the mayor's office are working on it," they'd say, knowing the political dynamics in the city were confounding.

I was about to head home for a few hours' sleep before my morning briefing, when my phone rang. It was civil rights attorney and activist Nekima Levy Armstrong, who I had gotten to know better over the past five years. I knew that if Armstrong was calling me near midnight, the news was not going to be good.

My apprehension was rooted in experience. My mind flashed back to November 15, 2015, when this scenario had played itself out in reverse. Just after 11:00 p.m., I had received a text message alerting me that an MPD officer had shot and killed Jamar Clark. Before I left for the scene, I called Nekima Levy Armstrong. I wanted her to hear this from me, and not on the morning news. I considered this not a diversion but a deposit in the goodwill account we had begun to build together—even when we found ourselves on opposite sides of a protest line.

Although it's unconventional for a police chief to have such a rapport with an advisor to Black Lives Matter, Armstrong and I had maintained an open line of communication over the years. She didn't have to call me that night of May 25, 2020, but she did.

I answered the phone: "Rondo here."

"Chief Arradondo," Armstrong said, "I've just been tagged in a Facebook post by a member of the community. Did your officers kill someone tonight?" Confused, I told her they had not. However, a person had died as he was taken into custody. Armstrong pushed back. "Well, the community is saying your officers choked someone, or crushed their throat. Have you seen any video? Because the community's version of events differs greatly from what your officers told you."

The in-custody death incident had occurred at the intersection of Thirty-Eighth and Chicago, just blocks from my childhood home. My alma mater, Roosevelt High School, is just a mile away. I still have cousins, aunts, uncles, and childhood neighbors who live in the neighborhood. For more than three decades, the intersection has been home to Cup Foods (recently rebranded as Unity Foods), the kind of corner store where kids stop for snacks and candy after school. Locals drop by for cigarettes, phone cards, or batteries. Sadly, in a city that has too many food deserts, many in the community have to rely on convenience stores for the basic essentials, but the choices offered are not the healthiest. This corner store at least sold fruits and vegetables. Down the block, there was a BBQ joint, a laundromat, a gas station, and a deli. For forty years, Pastor Curtis Farrar has held Sunday morning worship at his storefront church across the street.

Thirty-Eighth and Chicago has gone through an urban metamorphosis. It was a central hub in the 1950s, '60s, and '70s that had the local market, pharmacy, soda shop, appliance store, laundromat, and church. It was also one of the city's busiest bus transit hubs. In the 1980s, the neighborhood changed greatly as the crack cocaine epidemic hit the city hard and the street gangs began to take hold. Thirty-Eighth and Chicago was the street territory of the Rolling 30s (30s indicates the avenues of control). Incidents of violence increased throughout the decade and into the 1990s. When the front line of the war on drugs reached Thirty-Eighth and Chicago, many of the gang leaders and their members were sent to prison, serving long sentences that left a vacuum and void of leadership. Young, unstructured gangs developed but didn't last as long or have the same impact. What occurred next shifted the nature of the neighborhood significantly: gentrification. A police officer today would consider the area challenging and yet understand that a lot of good people live there, just wanting to make a living and raise their families.

Earlier that day, I had reviewed the incident reports describing what had taken place at Thirty-Eighth and Chicago as a medical emergency. Before I could even wrap my head around Nekima Levy Armstrong's new and contradictory information, she called me again. This time, she sounded rattled and, more worrisome, expressed a sense of disbelief. Armstrong has experienced much in her life. When I sensed disbelief from her, I braced myself for the worst. She said, "Chief, your officers choked a man to death."

Through social media, Armstrong had just received the now-famous bystander video, shot by teenage eyewitness Darnella Frazier, that documented George Floyd's death. As Armstrong sent me the video on my cell phone, I was sitting down at my desk. I watched the video for the first time, and my stomach sank. I found myself squinting at the screen. The video's images were clear, but I squinted to try to will the video to stop showing me the absolute inhumanity I was seeing.

I have always tried to protect my own children and shield them from disturbing images, yet I knew I was going to be powerless to protect America's children from what they were about to see. Even worse, there wouldn't be any way to explain the callousness of someone who wore the same uniform as me killing a defenseless man. I knew within moments of viewing the video that my life was going to change forever, and so would the city.

I recalled an event from my childhood. When I was a young boy, my late grandmother, a staunch and proud Baptist who attended church as if it were her second home, maintained three unique items in her living room: a gaudy, overly large velvet portrait of Jesus, a dish on her coffee table filled with what we called "old folks candy," and, next to it, a pristine decades-old copy of *JET* magazine, protected by heavy plastic. This last item, clearly treasured, seemed jarringly out of place in the otherwise comfortable room. The famous yet gruesome picture of Emmett Till in his open casket was on the cover of the magazine. In the photograph, Mrs. Mamie Till stood over her son's body with an agonized look on her face as if silently crying out from the magazine, "Why?"

I never understood why my dear grandmother kept a constant visual reminder of that horror in plain view in her living room. When I watched the video of Mr. Floyd's murder, it became clear to me. My grandmother was, in her own symbolic way, comforting Mrs. Till by letting her know: "While I may not be able to answer why you were made to suffer, I can promise you I will *never* forget your grief and I will make sure my children and grandchildren never forget your grief either."

Darnella Frazier's video changed the course of history by making all of us witnesses to a crime. In this new age of social media, we could no more turn away from it than I could turn away from that *JET* magazine cover. Frazier's courageous documentation revealed an incontrovertible truth that many, nevertheless, would later dispute—including the president of the Minneapolis Police Federation union. This was murder, committed in broad daylight.

There is a chilling, surreal quality to the video. I watched George Floyd's fear escalate as he realizes he is defenseless. I saw the moment Mr. Floyd seemed to understand he was going to die in the street. When I heard this grown man cry out for his mother at the end, my heart shattered. I also understood that Derek Chauvin, the officer with his knee on Floyd's neck and back, had the power to stop this from happening. At any moment, he could have removed his knee. Even after Mr. Floyd became unconscious, Chauvin could have engaged the off-duty firefighter, standing steps away on the sidewalk, to help resuscitate him. Instead, he made the choice to continue, consciously but casually, toward the inevitable outcome. Why? He has never said, and we may never know. I have never met Chauvin, nor had the chance to ask him.

What struck me about Chauvin's aggression and persistence is how at ease he seemed, convinced that George Floyd did not deserve to live. At the beginning of the encounter, there may be a power dynamic layered over the biases that drove him. Perhaps he was flexing his might for the rookie officers accompanying him on patrol that day. But even a bully will usually walk away when he knows he's won. Bullies enjoy a little fight. Once they know their victim is in fear and will no longer resist their attack, they'll move on. That did not happen here. After the first several minutes, what began as cruel turned even more sinister. Floyd was helpless. There was no fight in him. Bystanders were pleading for his life. There was no threat to Chauvin, but he continued to assert his will. He was relentless. He already knew the outcome and he chose not to avert it, but to prolong it for nine minutes and twenty-nine seconds. To me, that was depravity.

Complicit in Mr. Floyd's murder were the three officers—Tou Thao, J. Alexander Kueng, and Thomas Lane—who failed to intervene to stop Chauvin.

The video shocked the conscience of people around the world, but what we don't often talk about is that men and women who work in policing were traumatized when they saw it. Part of the fabric of this profession is a requirement to keep our emotions in check. Most officers have been to calls where they have witnessed the horrific things human beings can do to one another. But when a horror is committed by someone who wears the uniform, that is a deeper wound. The danger to the people is not supposed to come from us. That's not what we represent. When Derek Chauvin or any other officer kills a person ruthlessly and cruelly, it not only sets us all back; it's a betrayal that cuts to the core.

The paramedics loaded Floyd's slack body into the back of the ambulance and drove away. Before finishing their shift, the four officers received word that the suspect accused of passing a counterfeit $20 bill at the corner market on Thirty-Eighth and Chicago had been pronounced deceased at Hennepin County Medical Center.

Throughout the department, officers would relay to their partners that if they were ever seriously wounded in the line of duty, they were to be driven immediately to HCMC. Their ER teams were called Dr. Frankenstein; they could bring anyone back to life. I can only imagine what was going on in the officers' minds when they were told that the original counterfeit call they responded to—and spent less than an hour on—resulted in the death of this man. I wonder if they understood it would ultimately change their lives forever, as well.

Once an in-custody death occurs, we activate MPD critical incident protocol. After receiving the report from HCMC, the four officers responded to City Hall, where they gathered in a designated room bustling with MPD personnel. Chauvin and the witnessing officers, Thao, Lane, and Kueng, were required to provide a short public safety statement documenting what occurred. As standard procedure, a forensic photographer took pictures of them in their uniforms. Department investigators also took possession of their body-worn cameras to be transferred to the Bureau of Criminal Apprehension. During this process, the four officers had the support of Police Federation union representatives and a Police Federation attorney. As I recall, that evening the process, from start to finish lasted a couple of hours. This was not unusual, especially because at that time no information had been revealed as to the specific actions of Officer Chauvin. The officers' reports stated only that, "The subject was resisting. He seemed high, and we had to restrain him. He started to pass out and we called an ambulance."

None of the witnessing officers called Chauvin out for what he had done.

I have been asked if the two newer officers should have "gotten a pass" from any discipline because we all know they were never going to speak out against a veteran Field Training Officer. I have known better since 1992 when I spoke the truth to an assistant county attorney, despite the risk to my career. So my response to that question was that our department policies are not based on years of service. There is not a special section in our policies that solely applies to the chief, nor one just for commanders and another just for Boots. We are all required to abide by the policies, regardless of rank or seniority, and the policy requires officers to intervene when a person's safety is threatened. If the two newer officers didn't feel they could intervene at the scene (despite the fact it's required) then, at the very least, they had an opportunity to speak up while meeting one-on-one with a Federation attorney. It would have been as straightforward as saying, "Officer Chauvin acted in a manner that I believe may have contributed to the individual's death and here is what I observed Officer Chauvin do."

If any of the other three officers had alerted anyone that Officer Chauvin possibly violated department policy that evening, there might have been a much different outcome for them. Mr. Floyd cried out for those officers to save his life. Watching the video, our sense of humanity screams at them to act. Yet those cries went unanswered.

In the officers' incident reports, the act of choking the life out of a man was simply noted as "applied restraint." I suspect when the officers got the news of Floyd's death, they reached for a version of events that was true enough to be defensible. They put information in the report that would explain their actions, but omitted critical details. Not one of them stated that Chauvin knelt on Mr. Floyd's neck for several minutes as he pleaded that he couldn't breathe— and bystanders pleaded, "You're killing him!"—before he became unresponsive. This was a grave and ominous omission.

That night around 10:00 p.m. I met with homicide detectives and a Police Federation representative to receive an update on the incident from the scene at Thirty-Eighth and Chicago. That was part of our critical incident protocol. I never met with the officers or had a conversation with them. During an active investigation, if I, as chief, ask the officers any questions related to the incident, it can be interpreted as a directive from their boss. A compelled statement triggers what is known as the Garrity

Rule, which basically says if an employee is compelled to provide a statement to his or her employer, that statement cannot be used against them in a criminal proceeding. During my tenure as chief, I never engaged in conversations with officers involved in critical incidents, knowing the seriousness of the legal implications associated with my role.

Along with my deputy chief of investigations, I did review video of Thirty-Eighth and Chicago from a pole camera across the street. But that camera was positioned in a way that only showed the officers' backs. From that angle, we did not see Chauvin kneeling on Mr. Floyd's neck. There were no other visible signs of violence. The bystanders on the sidewalk did not appear agitated. There was no audio from the pole camera, so we couldn't hear their remarks to the officers, which would have told us otherwise. We observed that at no point did Officer Thao push back a bystander, draw his mace, or struggle with the people on the sidewalk. Officer Thao appears to be calmly standing there.

According to the critical incident protocol, I turned the officers' body-worn cameras over to the Bureau of Criminal Apprehension, which has sole chain-of-custody of the footage. The MPD does not view the body-worn camera footage when the BCA is the investigating agency. In the past, communities felt the MPD had not been transparent when conducting their own review of critical incidents and had advocated for this checks-and-balances measure. In the coming days, the body-worn camera footage would offer a shift in perspective that transformed our understanding of events. But that night, we had observed nothing concerning in the pole camera footage or the officers' reports. Like everyone else in attendance, I left the briefing thinking nothing was out of the ordinary except that a tragic medical emergency had occurred. When I briefed Mayor Frey, he expressed sadness for the deceased and appreciated my update.

Reflecting on how events unfolded rapidly overnight and into the next day, I still think about how much worse it would have been had Nekima Levy Armstrong not chosen to call me, and how historically critical it was that Darnella Frazier had the wherewithal to film what took place.

Frazier's video immediately reminded me of Eric Garner, another Black man whose last words, as he died at the hands of a New York City police officer, were, "I can't breathe." Like Mr. Floyd, Garner died of neck and chest compression and prone positioning during physical restraint. His 2014 killing was captured on video and focused national attention on racial bias and use of force in policing. Specifically, it proved the lethal consequences of the type of restraint that had just been used by Derek Chauvin in Minneapolis—despite training and policies in place to prevent it. (The NYPD banned choke holds in 1993, MPD in June 2020.)

NYPD officer Daniel Pantaleo, who used a prohibited choke hold that killed Garner, was never criminally charged. He spent five years in desk duty limbo, still on the force and suing to keep his job. He wasn't fired until a judge's ruling in 2019 led to his termination by the NYPD chief.

The minute I saw the bystander video, I made the decision to fire Chauvin, Lane, Kueng, and Thao immediately. There are absolute truths in life. Among them: We need air to breathe. It is an absolute truth that the killing of Mr. Floyd was wrong. I did not need days or weeks or processes to tell me that.

Police chiefs and commissioners around the country serve in positions of authority and responsibility when lives hang in the balance. When crises arise, they must act quickly, honestly, and decisively. Indecision may seem like a friend in a moment of crisis, but it's truly an imposter. It will surely bring the leader and his organization thorns instead of the flowers they seek. Most citizens don't expect perfection from their leaders, but they do demand prudent and principled decision-making that results in action.

I had to act quickly. The clouds of chaos were gathering. In the morning, the fractious and intractable city council would weigh in. The city attorney would do what city attorneys are supposed to do—warn of our lawsuit liabilities. The national media would descend on Minneapolis. The Police Federation union would, almost certainly, circle the wagons around four of its own. Mass protests were inevitable. The 850 sworn MPD employees who reported to me would expect to know: What will happen to the officers involved?

And there was a decent chance I could be fired. I had a fleeting head start to do whatever was in my purview as chief to ensure that, when the sun rose on Minneapolis, the wheels of justice were rolling in the right direction.

I know that in times of great challenge and great distress, there must be calm. I have seen well-intentioned people make critical mistakes when strong feelings supersede good judgment. It was clear to me that after May 25, 2020, every word I spoke and every action I took was going to be watched closely by all. I had to be of clear mind and provide a steady hand in a time of turmoil. I am not immune to grief or trauma, but to lead through a crisis I must compartmentalize my feelings and deal with the situation at hand. Although the world seemed to freeze when I viewed the bystander video, the reality was that crime in the city hadn't stopped. Babies were getting shot, carjackings were multiplying, people were waiting so long for a 911 response that they were starting to lose faith that anyone would come. The city still needed the MPD.

I went into operational mode. I felt that Mr. Floyd, our community, the members of the MPD who dedicated their lives to honorable service, and, quite frankly, the country deserved accountability.

I picked up the phone.

Rainer S. Drolshagen, the special agent in charge of the Minneapolis bureau of the FBI, answered after several rings. He was new to the Minneapolis FBI field office, and we didn't really know each other. But I needed his help. I immediately felt that Chauvin and the other officers had violated Mr. Floyd's human and civil rights. That made the officers' actions a Federal crime.

"Special Agent Drolshagen," I said. "This is Chief Arradondo. I need you to scramble your agents *now* to Thirty-Eighth and Chicago." Drolshagen hadn't seen the bystander video, but I'm sure he knew from my voice how urgent I felt this was.

I was acutely aware that historically—like after the death of Eric Garner—accountability often evades the reach of departmental regulations and state laws. Without the Feds, we would be relying solely on a historically questionable statutory apparatus to bring justice for George Floyd. It wasn't a good bet.

Frankly, I also wanted to put a safety net in place, in case the mayor said to me the next day, "Rondo, nice working with you but don't let the door hit you on the way out." If the Feds had already spun up their own investigation, it wouldn't matter as much what political winds prevailed in the city. Even if a new chief decided to close ranks, the Federal investigation would not go away.

I had to rely on Drolshagen. I had to trust that he would get involved as soon as I asked, and would see it through to the end. In a groggy, just-awoken voice he said, "Rondo, if you are calling me at this hour, it ain't good." He took me at my word and pledged to send in agents immediately.

Early the next morning, Drolshagen came to my office and pledged his steadfast commitment to the Federal investigation. He had spoken to FBI Director Christopher Wray, and they would be handling this as a civil rights case. From then on, Drolshagen would be working closely with me, and the FBI would spare no resources. We both acknowledged some of the difficult history of the FBI when it comes to Black lives lost, but Drolshagen was clear that what happened in the past was not going to happen here.

My next call that night was to Mayor Frey. I could hear the concern in his voice when he sensed that I was treating this like a possible criminal act, as opposed to a good-faith mistake made by an officer. He told me he and his office would provide whatever support I needed, asked that I keep him updated, and said he would be in City Hall early that morning.

11

When Thirty-Two Was Thirty-Six

IT HAD BEEN FIVE HOURS SINCE GEORGE FLOYD DIED. SLEEP WAS OUT OF THE QUES-
tion. I reached in my desk and grabbed a handful of what my team
came to know as "Rondo's fifth food group," peanut M&M's, to
give me a sugar boost. I had more calls to make. Thirty-two, to be
exact.

One by one I dialed the leaders of the Minneapolis Black
community. The public notification of George Floyd's death had
begun with misinformation supplied by my department. I would
have some explaining to do. From the beginning, I was determined
that the pillars of the Black community would learn about George
Floyd's murder and its investigation from me, directly and personally.
I invited these leaders to a meeting at 8:00 a.m. in my conference
room at City Hall. It was the middle of the night so I mostly left
voicemails, hoping they would come.

I started with the bishops, reverends, and pastors. Nothing moves
in the Minneapolis Black community without the Black church.
Next, I reached out to the presidents of the Minneapolis NAACP

and Urban League. I called Elder Spike Moss, a freedom fighter from the civil rights era who fought for the integration of the Minneapolis police and fire departments. And, of course, I texted the community organizer I knew would also be awake and already mobilizing: Nekima Levy Armstrong. I also called young activists who were leading the Black Lives Matter movement in Minnesota. I made thirty-two phone calls that night and I did not start a single one by introducing myself. Most of those relationships dated back years, if not decades. We need each other in times of crisis, but alliances should not be transactional or transient. You can't expect people to support you if they don't know you.

By the time I finished the calls, dawn was breaking, and media satellite vans had begun to gather near the arched stone entrance to City Hall. I threw on a clean-and-pressed blue uniform shirt from the few I always kept hanging in my office cabinet. I had not slept at all. I washed my face and brushed my teeth in the office bathroom and walked down the hall to the chief's conference room.

Of the thirty-two people I invited to the meeting, thirty-six showed up.

We gathered under the fluorescent lights, taking seats around the square table. Immediately to my right was Nekima Levy Armstrong. NAACP president Leslie Redmond sat next to her. Bishop Richard Howell was to my left at the head of the table, along with Reverend Babington-Johnson. At the other corner was Elder Spike Moss. Across from him was BLM activist Raeisha Williams. Some people walked into the room in tears. Others were just hearing what had happened and hadn't yet seen the bystander video. Not all the people in that room got along. Some who had different points of view found themselves seated directly next to each other. But at that moment, you could not tell who might have disagreed with one another in the past.

Once everyone was seated, we locked the door.

The one person I had not informed about this meeting was the mayor. I hoped this breach of protocol would not damage our good relationship, but I felt it was necessary. I knew that in the coming hours, the filaments of politics would penetrate the dialogue on George Floyd's murder and its significance for our city and our country. As a child of Minneapolis, I felt an obligation to speak unvarnished truth to the leaders in that room, without the veil of cautious diplomacy that would descend if my boss were sitting next to me. That meeting needed to be intimate, raw, genuine. Another member of the Black community had lost his life, and this was between us.

Of course, the presence in City Hall of thirty-six Black leaders in various states of distress did not go unnoticed, nor did the media amassing outside. I'm sure the mayor wondered what was going on and would have appreciated visibility to the discussion in that conference room. He tested the waters by dispatching an aide to knock on the door. I unlocked it, and one of us stepped into the hallway to inform the aide as politely as possible, "Nobody else is coming in. Not even the mayor."

Like every other person in that room, I was hurting, grieving, and seeking comfort. I asked Bishop Howell to begin the meeting with a prayer. Dressed in a formal jacket, Bishop Howell stayed seated but asked everyone to bow their heads. He called for a blessing for the life that was lost. He called for a blessing for our city, the strength to move forward, and for peace. "Dear Lord," he said, "please guide our chief."

I began to speak. Every person in the room went silent and leaned in. I let them know, as chief, that I couldn't promise them I knew how this was going to unfold. And I was going to need their help. We were headed into uncharted territory. There would be forces in play that none of us may have encountered before in our lives, not even the elders.

I gave a rundown of what occurred from the moment the call came out from Cup Foods around eight thirty the previous night, to what happened when Nekima Levy Armstrong called me, to the role the FBI would play. I shared that MPD homicide investigators were already on the job and would be shadowing the Bureau of Criminal Apprehension. I apologized to every single person in the room that the MPD's initial report of a medical emergency was false and had created distrust.

I felt the gravity of the crisis and I didn't want to let these leaders down. The young people in that room were already pouring their energy and abilities into building a more just and equitable city. Many of the elders had protested for our civil rights in the very same corridors of City Hall that now housed my office. Many had fought hard over the years so that someday there might be a Black chief of police. There was a part of me that felt crushed, wondering if they were thinking that, although they had lived long enough to see the day when a Black chief ran the Minneapolis Police Department, they had also lived long enough to see the most horrific act that a police officer could do to a citizen in the city— and it had happened on my watch.

As I struggled to reconcile this paradox, I made a promise to myself that the very minute my staying on as chief created more harm and trauma for this community, I would turn in my badge to the mayor. I silently pledged to use every second I had left in this job to make a difference, to keep bringing hope to the table, and to uphold the truth.

At the same time, in that group more than any other, every person knew the line I walked, reporting to the mayor and beholden to the city council. Some of us shared an unspoken prediction that many of the council members who had been waiting in their starting blocks had just heard the gun and would be sprinting as fast as they could to defund and dismantle the MPD.

Everyone around the table wanted to know what I was going to do with the officers involved. I knew I was going to terminate all four of them. However, I still needed to hear from the community what they believed and what they thought. Some said, "Fire all four officers immediately." Some even said, "Rondo, we understand if you are only able to fire the one officer." They knew that to hold the witnessing officers accountable for their complicity would be a step beyond what had ever been done before. Even at that moment, they still wanted to protect me from the fallout. But I was willing to go as far as necessary. As a leader, I believe that what you permit, you promote. There was no way I was going to endorse or excuse the failure of Thao, Kueng, and Lane to intervene.

I told the assembled leaders that although I was bound by human resources policies limiting what I could say about personnel matters, I was nevertheless going to walk out of that meeting and go straight to the microphones now bristling on the steps of City Hall. I would declare that those four officers were no longer employed with the Minneapolis Police Department.

Minutes later, I did.

But before I left the conference room that morning, we discussed the other critical issue at hand: How could we protect our community, and especially our children, in the coming days and weeks? We knew that the powder keg had just been lit, and yet we needed peace. The shared sentiment was that emotions are valid, but we couldn't let anger burn our city down and inflict more trauma on a community that had already suffered so much.

Many around that table had been warning for years that if the city didn't get a handle on economic equality and support our collective efforts at police reform, Minneapolis would become the next

Ferguson. Most of the leaders in that room had protested at some point during the tense and volatile eighteen-day occupation outside the 4th Precinct following the death of Jamar Clark. Since then, County Attorney Mike Freeman had publicly stated he believed Jamar Clark would still be alive if the officers had chosen other options. But based on the evidence, he declined to prosecute them. The $200,000 settlement Clark's family received from the city did not look or feel like justice to many in the community. The people carried Clark's memory forward as they went on to mourn Philando Castile, Justine Damond, and now George Floyd.

We heard the thunder rumbling, but we could not have predicted the scope and scale of the storm that followed. I never would have imagined that our united call for peace would not be echoed by all thirteen members of the Minneapolis City Council. None of us knew that by the end of the week, a five-mile stretch of Lake Street would be on fire and, across the city, more than fifteen hundred businesses damaged or destroyed—many of them owned by people of color. Today, even knowing how bad it got, I am convinced that without the unflagging collaboration and solidarity born in that City Hall conference room, it would have been much worse.

There was never a day in my thirty-two years in the MPD that I felt my community didn't support me. That doesn't mean we always agreed. But when I walked out of the conference room and stepped up to the podium that had been placed outside, I turned around and saw those thirty-six Black leaders of different ages, from different organizations, standing behind me vowing to help maintain peace in our city. The warmth that swept over me would carry me through the coming days, when the gathering storm broke over Minneapolis and the world.

12

No More Funerals

IN 2020, THANKS TO THE COURAGE OF A TEENAGER NAMED DARNELLA FRAZIER, A video of George Floyd's last minutes on Earth made its way around the globe, and we couldn't turn away. That video stood out from the accounts and footage of other police-related deaths, broke through the isolation of the COVID-19 pandemic, and pulled at our collective conscience, calling us to take a stand.

Law enforcement officers and agencies had to decide: Were we going to circle the wagons? Or would we declare in word and deed that what happened to George Floyd could not be defended or tolerated? Mayors, governors, and even the president had to take a stand. CEOs, celebrities, and athletes leveraged their platforms and influence. Americans left their homes for the first time in months to assemble in crowds, shouting George Floyd's name at protests in all fifty states.

A wave of denunciation circled the globe as protests swept through forty countries. George Floyd's photo—a selfie picturing his short-cropped hair and downcast eyes—appeared on protest signs from Beijing to Buenos Aires. His murder exposed the gap between American ideals of equality and the daily realities of many people of color in our society. Countries that the US had long chastised for government-sanctioned violence seized upon Floyd's murder as evidence of our hypocrisy. China, North Korea, and Russia posed the question: When millions of American citizens are taking to the streets to fight for their human rights, how can the US claim moral authority over other nations?

People around the world who had never heard of Minneapolis came to know the city as the epicenter of the global protest movement. Flowers, notes, drawings, and candles filled the intersection at Thirty-Eighth and Chicago. George Floyd's face—painted in stark black-and-white—looked down upon those tributes from a massive mural affixed to the bus shelter. Painted a few yards away on the pavement, near the spot where George Floyd died, a life-sized nude angel lay face down, arms behind his back—yet spreading his wings. On the wall of the corner store, the bright yellow halo of a giant sunflower framed Floyd's portrait. The site of the former Speedway gas station across the street was reclaimed as a community gathering space dubbed "The People's Way."

Three miles away, on the morning of May 26, 2020, I stood beneath a granite clock tower on the steps of Minneapolis City Hall, facing a row of reporters. I had just left the meeting of Black community leaders where I had promised to do everything in my power to hold Derek Chauvin accountable for George Floyd's killing and to hold officers Kueng, Lane, and Thao responsible for failing to stop it. I stood before the news cameras and announced on live TV that all four officers would be terminated from the MPD immediately. I made this statement without consulting the city attorney. I had only informed the mayor of my decision. He looked at me and said, "You have my full support, Chief."

Too often during a crisis, leaders will fail to act quickly and decisively. Instead, they try to hit a pause button that doesn't exist. They seem to understand that time is an enemy, but they don't realize that time always wins. You cannot buy time by deferring a difficult choice. Neither can a leader use a policy as a fallback, because at the end of the day, whatever has happened, you own it. If you try to avoid backlash by waiting to see which way the wind will blow, you cannot later claim that you acted on principle.

The reality is, some acts are indefensible. I didn't stand in front of those reporters to debate the facts we had all seen with our own eyes on video. Instead, I was there to uphold my values. Since the time I wrote my vision statement at that little kitchen table in 2017, I had made those values clear to all who reported to me: Honoring the sanctity of life is the most sacred of all our duties. My vision statement was not a philosophical exercise. I was communicating what would be rewarded and what would not be tolerated on my watch. I knew that the majority of officers would get behind this vision, or already subscribed to it. But I also knew that some would not endorse or uphold it. If those adversaries should reveal themselves through the use of excessive force, and if our paths should cross in a disciplinary hearing or court case, those officers would have no grounds to claim they were "just doing their jobs."

Firing all four officers was a dramatic departure from recent cases in cities where officers had killed or harmed Black Americans but kept their jobs and faced no discipline. Removing them from the MPD was a necessary first step on the path toward justice for George Floyd. There were many in Minneapolis who still carried the pain from the in-custody shooting death of Jamar Clark—and the lack of any repercussions for the officers involved. I hoped that firing all four officers I deemed responsible for Floyd's killing would send a strong ethical and moral message. I stood before the microphones and called the crime what it was: murder. Unequivocally. I knew decisive and meaningful action was required, but I also understood that my actions that morning would not be enough to dampen the outrage of the people. A crisis typically gets worse before it gets better. Floyd's senseless killing in Minneapolis reminded the world of the cruelty and depravity humans are capable of. I prayed we would soon realize the capacity for our better angels to rise.

In the waning hours of relative calm on Tuesday morning, I took the time to attend to a personal matter. I needed to pay my respects to George Floyd. I went with my deputy chief to Thirty-Eighth and Chicago. I knelt down, removed my hat, and said a private prayer. I thought about Mr. Floyd's family and their heartbreaking loss. I grieved for his six-year-old daughter, who would grow up without her father, and for his fiancée, who would never have the wedding she dreamed of. I would hold them in my heart throughout the challenges to come. I could not bring George Floyd back, but I made a silent promise to do whatever I could to bring him justice.

After the impromptu press conference, I spoke with FBI Special Agent in Charge Rainer Drolshagen, who had responded to my plea for assistance in the early hours of the morning. Drolshagen's agents were already on the ground conducting a Federal criminal investigation into the violation of George Floyd's civil and human rights. In the back of my mind, I understood that at any moment the mayor might decide to show me the door, so I wanted to ensure that the Feds received everything they needed from the MPD as soon as possible. If I did get fired, there was no guarantee the next chief would be so willing to cooperate with the FBI.

A few days later, I hurried from my car to my office to take a call from FBI Director Christopher Wray. The first thing he said to me was, "Rondo, how are you doing?" It was the first time during that tumultuous week I had heard such concern from an official, and it was genuine.

As we continued to talk, Wray confirmed that in too many cases involving a death in police custody, the police chief or sheriff wouldn't even think of reaching out to the FBI. We both acknowledged that the days ahead were going to be hard—but we were hopeful that, as a nation, we would get through this. Wray and Drolshagen would work toward justice through their channels, and I would work toward justice through mine.

Millions of others would demand justice by taking to the streets. As the saying goes, if you back a man up in a corner, he'll come out swinging. From Minneapolis to Philadelphia to Birmingham and beyond, the people were about to burst out of the corner and demonstrate their collective strength. An estimated 15 to 26 million Americans joined a protest in the summer of 2020, exercising their right of free speech. In Minneapolis, peaceful marches and rallies drew massive attendance.

Starting on Tuesday, May 26, the MPD experienced its second crash course on the modern tactics of protest, the first having been five years earlier during the eighteen-day occupation of the 4th Precinct following the death of Jamar Clark. That protest was disruptive, but also limited to a single city block. Such confinement would not be the case again. Embers of anger and pain had been smoldering ever since—and this time, the resulting fire would not be contained.

By and large, the mourners who visited Thirty-Eighth and Chicago remained nonviolent. By midday Tuesday, an estimated eight thousand people had gathered there. But with the speed of a tweet, groups of hundreds to thousands also assembled, sometimes simultaneously, in other locations—from downtown Minneapolis to the I-35W freeway to the North Side business district to the miles-long retail and residential corridor of Lake Street on the

South Side. Throughout the coming weeks, protests took place at all hours of the day and well into the night. From a police perspective, this meant that protests required the resources of all five precincts on all three work shifts. The multiplicity and scale of the protests was something we had never experienced before.

From the dawn of May 26, the people of the city went about their pandemic-disrupted routines with bated breath. Businesses let workers go home early. Citizens were shocked, seeking to understand the reasons behind the horror they had seen on video. I began to receive the first reports of angry people pelting officers and paramedics with rocks and bottles while they were responding to 911 calls. I had spoken to my AC, Assistant Chief Mike Kjos, about the need for mutual aid from police departments in St. Paul and the Minneapolis suburbs. By that afternoon, Kjos had issued the text alert that spun up the MPD command post at the city's Emergency Operations Center. The post was staffed twenty-four hours a day with planning, logistics, intelligence, and operations teams.

From the command post, we were able to leverage technology— including several hundred public safety cameras—to obtain situational awareness of what was happening in all parts of the city. Representatives of the Minneapolis Fire Department, Minnesota State Patrol, Hennepin County Sheriff's Department, and Metro Transit Police were present to coordinate a response. AC Kjos was my right hand throughout the summer. I couldn't have asked for anyone more capable, professional, and trustworthy.

While Kjos held down the fort at the command post, I delivered frequent status reports to my boss, Mayor Jacob Frey—a young, first-time mayor whose response to this crisis was being observed throughout the world. The mayor had the unflagging energy of the collegiate long-distance runner he once was. He rarely sat. He stood;

he paced. But I saw a physical change take place in Mayor Frey that week. In this time of crisis, the mayor stood still. He looked me in the eye, and listened. He carried himself with the gravity required in the moment. I saw a leader rising to meet the demands placed on him. He had been elected to the office two years before, but when I saw him that Tuesday, he had stepped into his role completely.

To get through the days ahead, the mayor and I knew we had to be on the same page and trust each other. There was no playbook for what we were going through. Mayors and police chiefs from other cities didn't call to say, "We dealt with this three years ago. Here's what you do next." The Federal government might respond to catastrophes like airline disasters, flooding, and hurricanes but in this case they didn't call to say, "Minneapolis, we've got someone on the phone right now and we're going to walk you through this upheaval."

Yes, we had disaster protocols. But they did not cover the unprecedented.

Tuesday evening, the level of violence outside the 3rd Precinct escalated as protesters damaged the perimeter fence, broke the windows of police vehicles, pelted officers with rocks and bottles, and sprayed graffiti. I authorized the use of pepper spray to drive back the crowd, preventing entrance to the precinct and preventing the theft of weapons from police vehicles.

Across the intersection, a man dressed head-to-toe in black and carrying an open umbrella walked past the AutoZone store as if on a Sunday stroll, casually smashing the windows with a hammer. Many viewed his actions as inciting the looting that followed. His unhurried demeanor seemed to say, "See, it's easy. Why don't you give it a try?" Cell phone video of this strange scene circulated in social media, helping investigators to later identify the "umbrella man" as a member of a white supremacist prison gang.

By Wednesday evening, the crowd outside the 3rd Precinct numbered in the thousands. Protesters smashed out the glass in the front door and threw bricks through the windows. At one point, protesters tried to pull an officer into the crowd. Across the street, looters ransacked the Target store, sloshing across floors that had been flooded by the building's sprinkler system, grabbing items from shelves to the sound of ringing alarms. Stepping through shards of broken glass, looters carried away everything from diapers to electronics. I heard dispatch on the radio, fielding terrified calls from Target employees who had barricaded themselves in a back office.

The looting spread up and down the block to other major retailers. Fires blazed inside the AutoZone, Aldi, Dollar Tree, Cub Foods grocery, and Target. A six-story affordable housing complex under construction was burned to the ground, costing the community 189 new apartments. Nearby, another apartment building was completely engulfed in flames, with residents stranded on the roof.

Along a two-mile stretch of Lake Street, similar scenes were unfolding—with dire consequences for the mom-and-pop shops, restaurants, hardware stores, nail salons, and other services that have long brought energy, culture, employment, and vitality to this diverse urban corridor. Many of the business owners most affected were people of color or new arrivals to our country who had poured all their resources into building their livelihoods here. These businesses operated on paper-thin margins and sometimes without insurance.

On the boarded-up windows of their panaderías, mercados, barber shops, and coffee shops, business owners spray-painted appeals for solidarity—"Black Lives Matter," "Justice for George Floyd"—hoping to be spared. But this did little to deter the destruction. The violence was like a living organism—feeding on anger and frustration and growing larger each night. The Spanish language radio station, the Somali pharmacy, the local diner, the public library, and all but one of the neighborhood supermarkets would be in ruins by the end of the week. The cost of damages on Lake Street was estimated at $500 million, but that was not the only area affected. Looting and arson spread to every major business corridor in the city of Minneapolis. In all, more than fifteen hundred businesses in the Twin Cities were damaged or destroyed.

The MPD was stretched too thin, even with assistance from the St. Paul Police and the State Patrol. With our officers outnumbered hundreds to one, we couldn't simply go arrest the four hundred people outside the AutoZone, even though they were committing a crime. I was limited in my ability to reinforce our numbers because our mutual aid partners were also swamped. The suburbs of Brooklyn Park and Brooklyn Center and the city of St. Paul were experiencing their own large protests. My cell phone rang with updates from AC Kjos: "St. Paul's off the hook now. They're rioting on University Avenue. Those fifty bodies they said they could send to us, now we've got ten." We needed more help. Wednesday evening I contacted the mayor and instructed MPD Commander Scott Gerlicher, whose thorough account of the civil unrest informs this retelling, to prepare a written request for assistance from the Minnesota National Guard.

Meanwhile, people from outside Minneapolis had started to arrive, some with dark motives. Residents discovered caches of projectiles and Molotov cocktails stashed in their neighborhoods. Investigations attributed these caches to organized groups that dispatch operatives when high-profile social injustices occur somewhere in the United States. Their purpose was *not* to seek accountability and justice but rather to hijack the cause and seize on the mass media attention to disrupt government and create instability and disorder.

Nekima Levy Armstrong called me from outside the 3rd Precinct to say, "Rondo, I'm out here and I'm telling you it's not good. I'm getting my people out of here before the sun goes down." Armstrong has been protesting for years and believes in protesting, but she knows that rage is a dangerous thing when it takes over a group or a crowd or a cause. The contagion of rage was as real as the contagion of COVID-19. And the focus of that rage was the Minneapolis Police Department.

Some in the community were seeing police officers only from the neck down. Everyone who wore the uniform looked the same to them and became the target of their disdain, verbally and physically—even if it meant impeding officers who were trying to save lives. I understood that people were angry, but I could not allow their anger to prevent my officers from giving medical attention to a person bleeding in the street. Assaults on officers were happening so frequently that I held a news conference. I assured residents that if they have problems with the MPD, we could talk about that—but you could not endanger your neighbors by obstructing a police response because you were angry.

I was extremely concerned because my officers were a target for those who directed their rage at the police. Dispatch was vetting suspicious 911 calls that could be a setup for an ambush. They did all they could to ensure that callers were not giving false addresses that would turn out to be an empty field or dark alley. The hate mail stacked up in the precincts and in my office, along with the bomb threats and anonymous voice messages that said, "Don't let me catch one of you guys alone." Our intelligence team was monitoring social media and receiving alerts from the Feds when they picked up credible chatter. All precincts were on high alert.

Theoretically, cops' jobs are high-risk every day. But in this situation, that was not an abstract threat. I was constantly worried that someone would try to make a point by assassinating one of us. It wouldn't require much for someone with a rifle to take their shot under cover of the massive crowds.

Just because there were protests didn't mean that crime had stopped in the city. Kia Boys were still jacking cars and racing them through the streets. Mothers in North Minneapolis were still moving pillows and blankets to the bathtub so their kids could sleep safe from gunfire. Homicides, domestic violence, and car crashes did not take a hiatus. Robberies and break-ins continued. The MPD was still accountable to answer those calls, and my officers were out around the clock. But it seemed to some like the police had disappeared from the neighborhoods. And there was a reason for that. We were spread so thin that we did not have enough units to respond to even "priority one" 911 calls—the most serious, life-threatening crimes or accidents. A ninety-minute snapshot from the night of Wednesday, May 27, illustrates our plight. At 11:26 p.m., six priority-one calls were marked "pending" because there were no units available to respond. By midnight, ten calls were pending. By 2:00 a.m., there were fourteen pending calls. Each of those fourteen 911 callers was seeking help for a serious accident or violent crime—but they would have to wait.

That same Wednesday night the Minneapolis Fire Department responded to more than thirty fires throughout the city. As I watched parts of my childhood neighborhood burn, I was reminded that fire can be dangerous and dangerously intoxicating. People were drawn close to the flames, seemingly unalarmed. More than anything, they seemed mesmerized. The burning buildings were also surrounded by angry onlookers, the roaring sound of fire punctuated by the pop of gunshots.

The fire chief couldn't risk sending his unarmed firefighters into harm's way without a police escort. If a store was on fire with hundreds of looters outside, that required hours of time from six to ten officers. But I had few officers to spare. The reality was, we couldn't cover every fire. The fire chief had to acknowledge that the city was going to lose buildings and structures. At this point, both our departments were triaging—and our shared priority was the preservation of life. Buildings can be rebuilt.

It was nonstop chaos. My phone rang at all hours. Native and Indigenous community leaders in the Little Earth housing community called to say, "Just to let you know, we're armed; we're getting reports there are bad characters out there and we're not going to let anyone in here who wants to harm us." The Imams alerted me that their men were also armed and positioned on the roofs of the mosques. Property owners wanted to know if the flames were going to reach their apartment buildings. But I didn't know if the arsonists were going to shift from burning businesses and take it up the block to residential areas. A lot of those conversations were about reassurance and hope, because quite honestly, that was all I had to give them.

We were outnumbered and under attack, but we couldn't quit trying. I felt that the city and its people needed me. My home base throughout those days was my unmarked SUV. I was rarely in one place for long. No sleep aside from a few cat naps on my office couch, my subconscious mind still attuned to every alert from my cell phone. I subsisted on my fifth food group, peanut M&M's. I brushed my teeth in the City Hall bathroom and tried to refresh myself by putting on clean shirts. If I was in my office for a quick minute, I would look at the picture of Henry G. Thompson.

I frequently stopped by Zion Baptist Church to brief faith leaders and community leaders. I was regularly in touch with young activists to discuss what they were experiencing during this ever-changing situation. I especially needed the community's help to try to counter some of the false narratives spreading on social media. One rumor was that the Minnesota National Guard had directives to shoot protesters and looters. This was untrue and dangerous, and spread as quickly as the arsonists' fires. I needed help from community members to extinguish both. If local activists put out a tweet, the protesters saw it. If the DJs at KMOJ radio shared a message, it would reach the communities that needed reliable information. I also regularly briefed the local and national media. I tried to infuse my updates with hope because nobody else was doing that.

The mayor certainly understood the importance of communicating to his city during this time. Unfortunately a majority of the thirteen-member city council would not stand with him to deliver a unified message urging peace in our city. When people burn mom-and-pop small businesses, who does that hurt? These businesses supplied jobs and essential services. When our city was struggling to provide resources for the unsheltered and an affordable housing development burned to the ground, it hurt us all. But when the city needed its council members to set aside their differences and join the mayor to call for calm, they were unable to step forward and say with one voice: "We can still talk about justice and about holding officers responsible, but fires, looting, and arson don't help our city—they harm our city."

What kept me going through sleepless nights and unrelenting pressure were phone calls from my son and daughter. Just hearing their voices comforted me. Like many parents, a part of my brain remained permanently dedicated to concern for their well-being. My children were young adults, but I still needed to know they were safe. Their words of support refreshed my sense of hope when I was weary.

On Thursday night, May 28, thousands gathered in downtown Minneapolis in a massive protest outside the Hennepin County Government Center. Some downtown businesses were looted, and officers were attacked with rocks and bottles. At the same time, three miles away at Lake Street and Minnehaha Avenue, the situation surrounding the 3rd Precinct was getting worse. Members of the crowd fired gunshots in the parking lot outside the wrecked Target store. Flames whooshed from the windows of Minnehaha Liquors across the street, searing the air outside the precinct.

I was alone in my car, parked about a block away on Minnehaha Avenue facing south. The looted Target was to my right, the burned-down AutoZone was directly to my left, and the precinct was front and center. This is my city, and I was not going to make critical decisions from a sanitized command post miles away. I had come to monitor the situation in person. Even with my car windows rolled up, I could hear the chants and the screams of protesters. I heard pistol shots being fired and, every now and then, automatic weapons and rifle fire in the distance. I smelled smoke and the distinct odor of burning rubber from the tires inside the AutoZone.

People were standing on the rooftop of Minnehaha Liquors as it burned. They held homemade Molotov cocktails, fuses lit. Streamers of flame flew across the street and the bottles smashed into the 3rd Precinct, shattering with a small burst of fire as they hit their target. The officers turned off the precinct lights to conceal their movements inside. As I listened to their reports over the radio, I could hear their apprehension growing.

Between fifteen and twenty officers, mostly SWAT team members, remained at the 3rd Precinct that night—some were barricaded inside and some were positioned on the roof. The sheer number of people surrounding them was astounding. A constant volley of rocks, bottles, debris, and paintball rounds struck the precinct along with the Molotov cocktails, sailing past the concrete barriers and concertina wire. Someone lit a fire outside the front entrance. SWAT officers stationed on the rooftop deployed flash-bangs, tear gas, and rubber bullets to drive back the crowd but their actions only seemed to fuel the rage.

The energy was a mixture of anger and suspended action. Something was about to happen. A crescendo was building. I knew with absolute certainty that lives were in danger—the lives of officers and civilians. Until this point, the crowd had been gathered in front of the precinct building. But some were now starting to peel off toward the rear of the building, where the only remaining exit opened onto a fenced-in parking lot. The crowd was hell bent on getting inside, regardless of who was in there. The protesters didn't know if there were twenty officers in that building or two hundred. It didn't matter. They were determined not to let them get out. The imbalance of power that for hundreds of years had weighed in favor of the police had been overturned. The officers were outnumbered by thousands. If I didn't act soon, the officers would be engaged in hand-to-hand combat with an angry mob. My options had narrowed to two choices: hold the precinct—risking the lives of officers and civilians—or evacuate. And I had to decide right then. My priority, and therefore my choice, was clear. I would do what was necessary to preserve lives.

When the crowd surged forward to try to break through the precinct doors, I knew the officers inside didn't have much time. I radioed AC Kjos and told him I needed an evacuation plan. He said, "I'll get back to you within an hour." "No," I told him, "I need it *now!*" Over the radio, I heard veteran officers speak in stressed, fearful voices from inside the precinct. "We gotta move!" they shouted. "They're breaching!" And they were. The doors of the precinct were no match for the force of the crowd. It was time for me to make the call that no chief ever wants to make.

Just before 10:00 p.m. on Thursday, May 28, I got the mayor on the phone and said the words that echo in my mind to this day. "Mayor, as your chief I can no longer keep our city safe." There was a pause. "I'm sorry, what did you say?" replied Mayor Frey. He heard me; he just couldn't believe it. I said it again. "I need you to make a formal declaration to the governor for National Guard assistance ASAP. We are overwhelmed. We cannot hold the 3rd Precinct." We quickly came to a decision. The mayor gave me the directive to clear out all police personnel from the building, and I immediately gave the order for the officers to evacuate.

When the emergency tone goes out over the radio, it pauses all other radio traffic. It's a Mayday alert. Wherever they are, at crime scenes or in squad cars, officers go silent. Dispatch hit the tone and my voice emerged from radios across the city. "We've lost the 3rd Precinct," I said.

At that moment, the front doors of the building gave way. A group of protesters rushed inside and immediately began destroying the lobby and lighting fires. Just seconds before, all officers who were inside had exited out the back, single file, dressed in their riot gear. But instead of escaping quickly, the officers found themselves trapped between the now-burning building and the tall chain-link fence that surrounded the parking lot. There was only one way out—and it was blocked. The gate had been padlocked from the outside. The people who locked it did not intend for those officers to leave—at all—or for others to help them. Several officers scrambled into police SUVs and one of the cars rammed the gate. The hinges snapped and the gate sprung open. A line of squad cars drove through, providing cover for the officers running on foot. Fireworks, projectiles, and jeers from the crowd filled the smoky air.

That night, the 3rd Precinct was reduced to ruins. It was heart-wrenching to watch. But not a single officer or civilian was killed. No officers were forced to fight their way through a fire, without hoses, when no fire trucks could get to them. The precinct held computers, files and records, personal lockers, and a secured armory where shotguns and ammunition were stored. Because the fire did such extensive damage to the entire structure, it's unclear what was looted and what was destroyed. What we know for sure is that no officers were injured. I had made a choice between bad and really bad options, and I would make that same choice today.

To some, the evacuation of the 3rd Precinct was a demoralizing failure. To me, the outcome was a miracle. To my knowledge, no other American police facility has been besieged like that, ever. Look at the video, and tell me who had the upper hand. The mere fact that we did not lose lives makes me believe we had luck or a higher power on our side.

Regardless of what the political posturing was during this time, my number one goal was no more funerals. The next day, President Trump weighed in on Twitter, "I can't stand back & watch this happen to a great American City, Minneapolis. A total lack of leadership. Either the very weak Radical Left Mayor, Jacob Frey, get his act together and bring the City under control, or I will send in the National Guard & get the job done right." Trump then escalated his position with this tweet: "these THUGS are dishonoring the memory of George Floyd, and I won't let that happen. Just spoke to Governor Tim Walz and told him that the Military is with him all the way. Any difficulty and we will assume control but, when the looting starts, the shooting starts."

We know now from the account of retired general Mark Milley that Trump requested ten thousand troops be deployed in the streets of Washington, DC, to quell protests there. Milley exercised moral courage and refused. I respect the principled decision he made. Milley was doing everything he could from a national perspective to avoid throwing accelerant on an already inflamed country.

Most importantly, this was not a wartime action. The MPD still had to operate under departmental policy, state law, and city ordinances. The Constitution was not suspended during the summer of 2020, unlike what some would like to think. I could not give orders to start opening fire on civilians. The police oath of office respects the rights of the people, and these rights had not been repealed. Imagine that the mayor had said, "Rondo, have your officers stay put and defend that precinct at all costs, even using deadly force." Imagine I had given that order to the officers. Now imagine that the bodies of dozens of civilians were strewn across the streets of Minneapolis the next morning, and a new video was circulating around the world. Or perhaps we would be watching footage of officers being shot or violently beaten.

There's no point in defending a precinct station if innocent civilians and officers die in that process. Sometimes, no matter what decision you make, there will be damage. So the question becomes: What can you survive? While I have always tried to keep the MPD apolitical, I have been criticized by the left and right for "abandoning" the 3rd Precinct. I would make the same decision today. I'm at peace with it. I'm willing to take the heat from the president of the United States or anyone else. I'll even take the heat from my own officers, although that is the most difficult.

After the evacuation, the officers from the now-destroyed precinct arrived at the rendezvous point, the Special Operations Center. Some officers were in tears. All seemed shell-shocked. Some may have felt they could have successfully held the precinct if given the chance. Some may have felt defeated, or even humiliated. Some might have been glad to escape with their lives. They all had been attacked, verbally and physically—and yet they had continued to show up to work. Now, they were the last officers who would ever report to that precinct building. Most had taken this job to serve the community, but now their kids and spouses were hearing bad things about the police from their classmates and coworkers. Some felt that neither the department leaders nor the community cared about them. I walked up to a senior officer I had known for many years and considered a friend. I could see he was deeply shaken. I tried to put my hand on his shoulder, but he shook me off and turned away. He couldn't even look at me.

That was hard to take. Even so, I have no regrets. I've been to enough police funerals and I refused to go to any more. Like the officers in that room, I've got family and I've been insulted on the streets and vilified in the press. I have to shake that off and look at the big picture. Structures burned, stores were looted, businesses were destroyed never to return again, our core business district of Lake Street will never be the same as it was before 2020. Today there are tributes to George Floyd throughout our city and rightly so. Everyone's life mattered to me. What *didn't* happen is just as important as what did. What we *don't* have along Lake Street is a single memorial for a person who was trapped in an arson fire and died. There is not a single cross marking a spot where an eighteen-year-old was killed during civil unrest. And we are not gathering during Police Week in May to remember Minneapolis police officers killed in the line of duty in 2020.

Friday, May 29, Governor Walz held a news conference rebuking President Trump's inflammatory tweet. Walz attributed Thursday night's chaos to the city's lack of leadership and declared that he would restore order to the city. "You will not see that tonight," he said referring to the arson and looting. But his claim turned out to be overly optimistic—even with seven hundred members of the

National Guard added to the streets, the destruction was worse on Friday night. On Saturday, Walz called in all the resources available to him, fully mobilizing the state's National Guard for the first time since World War II. It was the largest domestic deployment in the Minnesota National Guard's 164-year history.

When you're in the eye of the storm, you must focus and keep moving. I knew the loss of the 3rd Precinct was unsettling and upsetting to many of our officers, but we had work to do and I needed everyone to show up as their best selves. I sent an email to all MPD staff. "Please know that the MPD is not defined by brick and mortar or the uniform we wear but rather our character, soul, and love of service," I said. "We *will* move forward. During these unprecedented times, those we serve need us to be that beacon of light to guide them toward a hopeful tomorrow."

I called a meeting with my command staff at the Currie Public Works facility. As I got out of my car, a public works employee waved to me and called out, "Chief! Chief!" I asked him to please call me Rondo. The man said, "No. Me and my wife and kids live in North Minneapolis. So you're my chief, and that's what I'm going to call you." He asked, "Are you going to be around? I have something I want to give you." I told him I'd be in a meeting for a couple of hours. "No problem," he said. "I'll wait."

In the conference room upstairs, members of my senior staff were seated around a whiteboard. I stood up from the table and drew a triangle on the board. At the tip of the triangle I wrote "chief and administration." At the lower left corner I wrote "media and elected officials," and at the other corner I wrote "community." One at a time, I tapped the three points of the triangle and said, "The rank and file can blame me all they want. If they're upset, if they're angry, they can blame me." I tapped the left corner, then the right. "They can be unhappy with the media and the city council;

they certainly can be. Or unhappy with the community and what they're doing." Then, I pulled my chair back from the table and I placed my knee on the seat cushion to emphasize my point. In the middle of the triangle I wrote "9 minutes 29 seconds." I turned to my senior staff and said, "But if the rank and file do not direct any of their disappointment or their anger and frustration to what those officers did at Thirty-Eighth and Chicago, this city will burn again."

I believe that policing is a noble profession. That's why I must call it out when someone who wears the uniform commits a violation against humanity, even if that is unsettling for other officers. The response was emotional. There were senior officers in that room with tears in their eyes who talked about how their kids were being mocked and ridiculed at school because their parents were police officers. One commander was dismayed that his officers had been refused service at a downtown pizza joint when they were in uniform. "I understand," I said. "But we can't respond to disrespect in kind. We need to find our better angels. This isn't the time for us to lower our standards or abandon our values."

I needed my command staff to be models of integrity for the men and women who continued to put on their uniforms and come to work under unfathomable stress. I'd rather move forward with just a few senior officers who believed in our oath than many who nodded their heads but ignored the oath we made to the people.

"The days ahead will be the most trying days of our lives and the most significant time in your career as a police officer," I said. "I need you to go home and have a candid conversation with your loved ones. If you come back to me tomorrow and you say, 'Chief, I'm not up to it, I don't have enough gas in the tank to do this,' I will honor that. I will get you to another unit. For everyone who decides to show up tomorrow, I need you to be all in. If you stand with me and we walk this road together, we will get through this."

After the meeting, I walked back to my car and again heard a voice call out, "Chief!" The man who approached me earlier had stuck around past shift change to speak to me. He pulled out a piece of paper and he said, "Here's why I call you chief. I was a chief petty officer in the US Coast Guard." He handed me the piece of paper. On it was a drawing of an anchor and chain, the emblem of the chief petty officer. He said, "You got a couple of minutes?" I said yes. He said, "I need to read this to you." He then proceeded to read a description of the traits that a chief petty officer must live by. These traits are true for every leader. "The anchor is emblematic of the chief," he read. "It serves to remind chiefs of the responsibility they have to keep those that they serve safe from harm." The last trait he described was just what I needed to hear at that moment. "The chain fouled around the anchor represents 'the sailor's disgrace' and serves to remind a chief that there may be times when circumstances are beyond their control in the performance of their duty, yet a chief must still complete the task. It is during these difficult times that humility and fortitude learned ages ago at initiation or on bitter experience are brought to bear." He gave me the paper and said, "You'll always be my chief."

Somehow, in my darkest days, a stranger appeared in a parking garage to buoy my battered spirits. I'm sorry to say that I don't remember the name of the city employee who made such a difference to me that day. But I will never forget the words he shared with me.

13

The Union Grip

IN THE WINTER OF 2018, DURING MY SECOND YEAR AS CHIEF, THE REVEREND OF A North Minneapolis church texted me a photo. One look sent me barreling across the hall into the assistant chief's office, demanding, "I want the names of everybody who did this!"

The photo showed the lobby of the 4th Precinct. A few feet away from where the desk officer sits, someone had put up a Christmas tree decorated with a pack of menthol cigarettes, an empty can of malt liquor, police tape, a bag of Takis, and a cup from Popeye's fried chicken. AC Kjos looked at the picture on my phone with disgust and said sternly, "I'm on it, Chief."

Anyone who has ever worked with AC Kjos knows he does not suffer fools. As I walked back into my office, I overheard him very loudly telling the employee at the 4th Precinct that the tree *better not* still be in that lobby by the time he gets there.

Fifty years had passed since the 1967 uprising along Plymouth Avenue. Just three years had passed since the 4th Precinct had been occupied by protesters for eighteen days after the death of Jamar Clark. But the community's distrust in the MPD wasn't just rooted in the headline events. Antagonism is also born of the gradual accretion of diminishment and disrespect. Now here I was, staring at a display of racist garbage in full view of the community and everyone who worked in the 4th Precinct. How many officers had walked by that Christmas tree without voicing a complaint? Why did I have to hear about this tree from a member of the community? Where was the inspector and what on earth was he thinking when he permitted this tree in the lobby?

This rubbish brought a wave of shame to the MPD. Photos of the offensive Christmas tree spread through social media and soon made the news. I issued a public apology. "I'm ashamed and appalled by those who would feel comfortable to act in such a manner," I said. I felt the incident had set the entire department back and detracted from the positive progress we had made. It certainly proved there was much more work to be done. I immediately suspended the two officers who decorated the tree. After the internal affairs investigators reported their findings, I was able to fire both the officers. I also demoted the precinct inspector and transferred him to the traffic unit.

As soon as word of the tree reached the community, I received a call from Nekima Levy Armstrong, who had led the occupation of the 4th Precinct in 2015. She could potentially leverage her network to make us pay for this affront. Instead, she offered me restitution. That's the way she is. Armstrong is a warrior, and she was absolutely going to hold the MPD accountable. But she cares more about her community than anything else. So, when she saw a chance to restore pride and bring people together, that's what she decided to do. Armstrong informed me that she and other local activists would install an even bigger Christmas tree outside the precinct entrance. The spirit of Christmas would prevail, and they would show the MPD how it's done on the North Side. She also informed me that I would be attending their tree decorating event. I assured her I'd be there on time.

Neighborhood families brought festive ornaments, many hand-made by children, to decorate the new tree. This wholesome rebuke empowered the community and gave me a chance to apologize in person to the people we had hurt. The boughs were hung with candy canes, miniature sleds, and inscriptions of "peace" and "love." I lifted a small child up so she could place her ornament on a higher branch. I was thankful to Armstrong as I hung my own glittery star and spoke directly to the community members gathered around. "To each and every one of you," I said, "I want to say I'm sorry."

I now had to replace the 4th Precinct inspector I had demoted, and I knew that because we had damaged the fragile trust with the community, I could not simply promote the next person in line. I decided to do things differently. Not only did I personally interview every candidate who wanted to be the new inspector, I also invited a group of community members to interview each candidate and provide their feedback. It's the community's precinct and they wanted to hear what the new inspector was going to do differently.

Building relationships is how you make progress, and it's hard work. The new inspector would get the job only because they had the support of the community, and they would start out being accountable to the people. This is how the 4th was transferred into the capable hands of Inspector Kelvin Pulphus.

For the next two years, my decision to fire the two officers who decorated the tree was under arbitration by the Minneapolis Police Federation, the union that represents officers, sergeants, and lieutenants—around 770 members at the time. In the summer of 2020, nearly three months after George Floyd was murdered, the union arbitrator ruled that both officers should get their jobs back. By this point, one of the officers had retired, avoiding discipline. The second fired officer was placed back on the job. Mayor Frey protested in a statement: "The facts of this case are clear. Chief Arradondo's decision to terminate or discipline should not be overturned in cases like this. We need arbitration reform that tackles an arbitrator's authority to reinstate [fired officers] in cases of established, egregious misconduct."

It is reasonable for members of the public to question why any officer who has been fired for cause, or who has multiple complaints of misconduct, is permitted to continue to serve in the police department. I have the same question. During my time as chief, the union arbitration process overturned my disciplinary rulings about 50 percent of the time—and this rate of reversal was the same for the previous chiefs over the past ten years. The arbitration process even reinstated officers who had been terminated for excessive force. In one such case, I had fired an officer who was captured on video repeatedly punching an intoxicated, handcuffed Native American man in the face while the man was lying helplessly on his back on the sidewalk. Two years later, a union arbitrator reduced this officer's termination to a two-week suspension. There was nothing more debilitating to me, as chief, than when I had grounds to fire an officer for misconduct but was thwarted by a third-party process that returned that officer to patrol in our community.

Another thing I have always thought was counterproductive within the MPD was that the sergeants and lieutenants are in the same collective bargaining unit as the patrol officers they supervise. Other police departments around the country separate supervisors and rank-and-file officers into different collective bargaining units. Mayor Frey and I sought to do the same in Minneapolis. And here's why: Imagine you are a sergeant and you have reason to discipline one of your officers. But you know that if you try to impose that discipline, the officer will be represented by your own union if they choose to appeal. Who has your back? This conflict of interest helps break down the checks-and-balances that keep our communities safe. The frontline supervisors are in the best position to observe and address concerning behaviors. They may be able to take corrective action before minor issues escalate to serious violations, but they are not incentivized to do so. Now combine this flawed union model with an arbitration process that revokes discipline 50 percent of the time it is imposed. The likelihood of facing consequences for infractions is low enough that it can encourage officers to believe that "no one can touch us." Keeping this old model continues to stall meaningful culture reform within the MPD.

By the summer of 2020, I was fed up with the revolving door that prevented me from ridding the department of officers who had violated our oath and our policies. My internal standoff with the Minneapolis Police Federation became a public face-off on June 10 when I announced at a press conference that I was immediately withdrawing from contract negotiations with the union. I brought in advisors to conduct a thorough review of how the contract could be restructured to allow for true reform. From that day forward, the union "grieved"—that is, sent to arbitration—every disciplinary action I made until I retired. This included my termination of a sergeant who was caught on camera spraying a journalist in the face with pepper spray during the civil unrest of 2020. I fired him for egregious and unethical behavior, but he was able to remain on the job during the grievance process because of his veteran status, and he resigned instead.

My authority was often undermined by union leadership during that time because they did not see the value in accountability. Being liked by their members was more important than being principled.

My vision and values were incessantly challenged by the union president, Lieutenant Bob Kroll. Kroll and I were contemporaries, having both joined the department in 1989. Kroll was elected union president in 2015, two years before I became chief. Although our careers progressed in tandem, our values diverged from the time we were Boots. Kroll immersed himself fully and irreversibly in the insular culture of the MPD. He was ride-or-die for cops, no matter what. He took any criticism of the department as an attack and seemed to view police reform as a threat to his way of life. For years, Kroll griped and groused that nobody else understood what it was like to do this job. To him, the protests following Jamar Clark's death signaled only that "everybody seems to know our job better than us."

I understand that we all want to be respected for the work we do. Policing is a noble and honorable profession. But we don't take an oath, and even put our lives in danger, out of a selfish desire to receive applause and accolades for everything we do. Police officers are public servants. Sadly, over time, the word "servant" has lost its dignity—even though it's truly an honor to serve our community. However, Kroll seemed to believe that because he wore the badge, it gave him a certain status over others. He did not react well when that perceived status was challenged.

With his signature slicked-back crew cut and horseshoe mustache, Kroll looked the part of the hard-charging, old-school street cops he admired. Off duty, he could be seen wearing a MAGA-red "Cops for Trump" t-shirt. Long before that, he was alleged to wear a motorcycle jacket with a "white power" patch, as noted in the 2007 discrimination lawsuit against the department. As recently as 2020, Kroll confirmed his membership in the City Heat, a motorcycle club for off-duty police officers in Minneapolis and Chicago. Kroll told journalist Ruben Rosario that the club was "as clean as can be," but a 2011 report by the Anti-Defamation League, titled "Bigots on Bikes," found otherwise. The club has members who have "openly displayed white supremacist symbols," the report stated. These included "Proud to Be White" patches and Klan symbols. Of course, not every member wears these warped insignia, but the club's permissiveness toward these racist tropes is well documented. And I learned long ago from my parents that you can measure a man by the company he keeps.

Over the course of his career, Kroll racked up thirty-two complaints to the Office of Police Conduct Review and the Civilian Review Authority—and he has said this proves only that he was a hardworking cop. Kroll was named in numerous excessive force lawsuits. One such incident occurred in May 2004, and was upheld by the Minneapolis Civilian Review Authority (CRA). The record states that Kroll and Officer Wallace Krueger, both off-duty sergeants at the time, were driving in Krueger's personal vehicle when a group of people crossed the street in front of Krueger's car. As they walked by, one of the pedestrians spun around, hitting the hood of the car with his shoulder bag. Witnesses and victims testified that Kroll and Krueger leaped out of the car and assaulted that man and his friends. Kroll and Krueger were not in uniform and did not identify themselves as police. They pushed one man to the ground and kicked and punched him. Kroll kicked another man repeatedly in the face. The pedestrians filed a complaint for excessive force and inappropriate conduct. The CRA panel recommended discipline for both Kroll and Krueger; as a result, the Minneapolis Police Department suspended Krueger for 24 hours, and Kroll for 160 hours.

Kroll's mentality was evident in the Federation's statement responding to George Floyd's death: "Now is not the time to rush to judgment and immediately condemn our officers. We must review all video."

When I read this statement, I was incredulous. The entire world—including Bob Kroll—had *already* reviewed Darnella Frazier's video documenting George Floyd's slow and deliberate extinction under Derek Chauvin's knee. Kroll calling for "more video" was a slap in the face. He had an opportunity to calibrate his statement to the reality and gravity of the situation. He had a chance to declare that Chauvin did not represent what his union members stood for and should never again be allowed to wear the badge. Instead, Kroll fought to get Chauvin his job back. If there's ever a case study of the consequences of defending the indefensible, it's Bob Kroll.

Kroll doubled down on his defense of Derek Chauvin in a letter to Federation members that was leaked to the press and remains posted, in full, on Twitter and a number of news sites. Dated June 1, 2020, the letter read in part:

No one with the exception of us is willing to recognize and acknowledge the extreme bravery you have displayed through this riot.

Given the right numbers, the right equipment and your ability to use them would have ended this Tuesday night.

The politicians are to blame and you are the scapegoats.

Kroll did not acknowledge that the "rioters" had taken to the streets because of the documented actions of four officers who belonged to his union. Instead, Kroll blamed the civil unrest on the politicians, the media, and me—anyone but Derek Chauvin. He went on to refer to the protesters as "terrorists" and to scapegoat the victim by claiming George Floyd was a violent criminal. The Federation's message was loud and clear, and the community heard it.

I believe Kroll could have learned a lot from the Minneapolis police officers who defended the Lee family against a mob in 1931. Those officers also faced an angry crowd of thousands, night after night. They got their lunch handed to them many times. But regardless of what their personal feelings may have been, the officers of 1931 stood by their oath, they stood by their chief, and they did the right thing. I have not seen any historical record of the 1931 union president protesting police involvement in protecting the Lee family's rights and safety. But in 2020, when the eyes of the world were looking to Minneapolis to see what stand the police would take, Bob Kroll hung onto a distorted nostalgia for a time when citizens and elected officials would turn a blind eye to police brutality. Kroll failed to understand that for generations, even in the most unlikely circumstances, police officers have chosen to do the right thing—whether it was popular or not. He was looking to the wrong side of history for guidance.

The reaction from city leaders to Kroll's letter to the Federation was swift and uncensored. Mayor Frey tweeted, "For a man who complains so frequently about a lack of community trust and support for the police department, Bob Kroll remains shockingly indifferent to his role in undermining that trust and support." Former Minneapolis mayor R. T. Ryback pulled no punches, saying, "We've never had a person leading the Federation . . . who is as likely to provide comfort to someone when they do something wrong, who is as central to that toxic culture as Bob Kroll. Bob Kroll is a cancer on this police department and on this city."

Around the same time, a group of fourteen officers penned an open letter to the people of Minneapolis condemning Derek Chauvin and his actions. "Like us," the letter said, "Derek Chauvin took an oath to hold the sanctity of life most precious. . . . Derek Chauvin failed as a human and stripped George Floyd of his dignity and life. This is not who we are." While I respect this public statement, I can't help but wonder why, out of the entire organization, only fourteen officers felt courageous enough to speak out. Perhaps there are more who would have been willing to sign their names. I don't know how many were asked. But I do know that millions of people around the world were standing up against what Chauvin did. And I wish that instead of fourteen signatures, that letter had hundreds.

It was nearly a month before Kroll finally went on the record to tell reporters that what happened to George Floyd was "a tragic situation that should never have happened." Kroll didn't speak for every officer, but he had the largest megaphone. Kroll was elected and reelected overwhelmingly, and the numbers don't lie. Dues-paying union members put Kroll in office, and there was a cost to that. I can't explain why this happens, but people will often vote against their own self-interests. I challenge any of those voting members to explain how electing Kroll enhanced their wellness and professionalism or improved their relationship with the people they took a duly sworn oath to serve.

While Kroll's public statements added gasoline to the fire, I was doing anything I could to calm the city. I reached out to a young activist named Raeisha Williams. I had gotten to know Williams during the investigation of her brother's murder in 2018, and I knew she cared deeply about the community. I asked her to introduce me to other young people who might be able to help me. I was aware that I was asking Williams to put her credibility on the line with some of her peers. But I also knew we shared a goal to keep people safe. "Police accountability matters," I told her. "We're both trying to see justice move forward—and at the same time, we need to keep the peace." Williams agreed.

Young people led the movements for change in 1967, 2015, and 2020. But many of the young protesters did not want to be seen with the chief of police. Raeisha Williams arranged a meeting on a summer day in a private backyard. Because of their respect for her, a half dozen young men agreed to come. Williams said a few words of introduction and then she left, because this specific conversation was meant to be with, about, and for young Black men. We sat together in the yard and they eyed me with varying degrees of curiosity or skepticism. These were productive Black men, most under the age of twenty-five, who contributed to their communities and were respected for it. But all of them had felt disenfranchised and devalued in their relations with the police. They were connected to other young men in their networks and neighborhoods who had been incarcerated or involved in gangs. We had all seen what happens when young men who have had a tough start are disrespected and feel hopeless. This state of mind is like dry tinder, waiting to be lit. Yet the very men who most needed to hear a message of peace were the hardest for me to reach. I had come to ask for help.

I tried to address the group's doubt about my intentions by letting them know who I was. We went through the Minneapolis ritual of figuring out what distant relatives and other people we knew in common. I told them that I was proud to serve my community as chief. But my job was not all that defined me, and we might be more alike than it seemed. I've also got scars and bruises within me. I've also been devalued by others. Some people feel that someone who looks like me should never have been given the position I hold.

The young men spoke to me about the generational pain that had been passed down to them from their fathers and uncles who were not respected as men by the police they had encountered. This pain was compounded by their own experiences. They told me, "Chief, you said that you were going to do better. But we know the history and now we've seen what happened to George Floyd. Your promises are starting to ring hollow." They seemed discouraged and several wondered out loud if things would ever get better. "Right now, there's worldwide attention on this particular Black man's death," they said. "But what's going to happen a year from now when George Floyd isn't in the news?"

Change often begins with a conversation. I made the young men a promise. "I will do everything in my power to keep our community safe," I said. "And I will never lie. I'll speak the truth. If one of the people who wears the uniform does wrong, I will hold them accountable. I will work tirelessly to provide hope to you, and the other young men that you interact with, that there can be a better day. But I can't do it alone."

These young men were also guardians of our communities and they did not want harm to come to them. "We don't want to see our neighborhoods destroyed," they said. "We're telling our networks not to burn our Black businesses or damage our stores. But there are thousands of people out there every day, and we don't speak for everyone." Still, they would do what they could to bring the temperature down. I was thankful for that.

At the same time, I was working to bring the temperature down within the MPD. Kroll was exploiting people's darker inclinations. He knew what he was doing when he conveyed to the rank and file that nobody wanted us, so you had better look out for yourselves out there. But I had to model the standards that I needed our men and women to meet, even under extreme duress. I needed their professionalism to rise above Kroll's combative rhetoric. I made my expectations clear to all officers: Don't denigrate people, don't alienate people, don't make offensive statements toward people because they do something you don't like.

During a crisis, the human condition will allow people to fall below standards. People will start to justify things that are out of bounds. And that happened during the civil unrest. Perhaps the most egregious incident was when a group of officers, riding in an unmarked van, beat up a blameless citizen named Jaleel Stallings. I learned of the assault only when Stallings filed a lawsuit. It wasn't an accident that nobody shared information up the chain of command to my desk. It was an example of some officers circling the wagons and abandoning our ethics.

Everything I did was watched closely by the rank and file who were looking to me for direction. As much as I wanted Kroll out of the department, I had to tread carefully. The last thing I wanted was to defy my own directive of respectful behavior. That would only give Kroll a sound bite for his propaganda and lead even more officers off the cliff. I could not make this fight public. But I was working hard behind the scenes.

I met with the mayor to figure out a legal off-ramp to remove Kroll from the picture. In early- to mid-June, I called Kroll privately to make him an offer. I was trying to appeal to his better angel, if it existed. "If not for yourself," I told him, "if you just want to do right by the department, I hope you'll listen to what I say next. Nothing good is going to come to the MPD as long as you remain on the job. We're at an inflection point. It's time for you to do the right thing and retire. I've talked to the mayor and city attorney, and we can offer you a financial package for your retirement. I'm urging you to take it." I was asking him to swallow his pride, and I knew I would be required to do the same. "I will even join you at a podium tomorrow for the announcement," I said. I was willing to take a hit to my own reputation to stand next to Kroll, because ultimately it wasn't about me. It was about the 430,000 people who were watching our city get torched.

"I need to connect with you tomorrow," I told Kroll. "You don't have days to think about this." Kroll agreed to go home and discuss the offer with his wife. The one glimmer of hope I had after that conversation was that he didn't immediately shut me down. He could have said, "F— you, I'm not going to step down." But he had agreed to consider it.

I called Kroll again the following day and told him I needed an answer. Kroll had thought about our conversation and discussed it with his wife.

"But," he said, "here's why I can't do it . . ."

I felt a sinking disappointment.

Kroll asked me to listen to a voicemail he had received the night before. It was a message from an officer that appealed directly to Kroll's Achilles' heel—his ego. The message was mostly profanity. "F— the chief, f— the mayor, f— the city council, f— the city," this officer said. "We need you to stick it to them. That's why we need you here."

Kroll told me, "That's why I'm going to stay."

I tried to reason with Kroll. "You're making this decision based on a message from someone who is shortsighted," I said. "You will be judged on the actions you took during this time in history. And when that judgment day comes, this officer will not be there to explain to your kids why their father is viewed as a villain and not a hero."

As it turned out, that officer left the department soon after my talk with Kroll. But it was too late. There was no changing the union president's mind.

Kroll thought he was standing strong, but I've seen firsthand that no one respects strength if it isn't based in humanity. Strength can be recognizing that what you are doing is harming others. Strength can be stepping aside. In the end, Kroll's stubborn brand of strength cost him the very things he cherished: the adornment of the uniform and all that comes with it. His badge was his identity. But Kroll failed to realize that the things he valued most were given to him by the people—and they could also be taken away. What I didn't know at the time of our conversation was that a dedicated group of community members was pursuing another strategy to unseat Kroll.

On May 26 and 27, 2020, Nekima Levy Armstrong gathered first aid supplies, helmets, and other gear to help protect the peaceful protesters from tear gas and rubber bullets. Near the precinct building, demonstrators were throwing rocks and bottles. But Armstrong was standing farther back and peacefully demonstrating when she was tear-gassed. Armstrong posted a Facebook Live video to let people know what was going on. She saw protesters around her bloodied by projectiles and choking from the chemicals in the air, and she felt it was a dangerous situation.

After viewing Armstrong's Facebook video, representatives of the Minnesota ACLU invited her to join a class action lawsuit against the city, filed by the ACLU and the law firm Fish and Richardson. The suit alleged that Minneapolis police used unnecessary and excessive force to suppress people's First Amendment rights to assemble peacefully and speak out against injustice. The courts combined multiple suits and, in the end, Armstrong was one of twelve plaintiffs. In November 2022, the city approved settlements totaling $600,000.

Bob Kroll was also named as a defendant in the suit *Armstrong v. City of Minneapolis.* "We hoped to stop Kroll from continuing to do more harm to the residents of Minneapolis, particularly residents of color and people who are most vulnerable," Armstrong told me, years later. "And we thought it was important that he no longer be a part of the force." The complaint alleged that:

> Kroll's position as president of the Federation "ampli-fy[ies] significantly" the supervisory role he plays in the MPD, and that Kroll "acts as an unofficial policymaker within the MPD." It is alleged that Kroll, "a de facto pol-icymaker for a cadre of officers" in the MPD, "actively sows discord between rank-and-file officers and the command structure as a means of further amplifying his policy role and exercising an outsize[d] influence over police culture."

The suit cited Kroll's June 2, 2020, letter to the rank and file as evidence he was functioning as an unofficial policymaker. Kroll claimed he "had numerous conversations with politicians at the state level" and had provided a Minnesota senator with a plan for National Guard deployment. The plaintiffs also alleged that Kroll's letter "sowed discord," was dismissive of peaceful protesters' rights by defining all protesters as "rioters," and encouraged the aggressive conduct of the MPD. Kroll's letter to the officers contained this example: "I commend you for the excellent police work you are doing in keeping your coworkers and others safe during what everyone except us refuses to call a riot. . . . The politicians are to blame and you are the scapegoats."

Kroll's letter referred to the protesters as terrorists—but for many years, community members had felt terrorized by Kroll, as evidenced by the complaints filed against him. The decision to sue Kroll was a new strategy in an ongoing battle by activists to remove him from the MPD. In the summer of 2020, Armstrong and hundreds of other activists held demonstrations outside the Police Federation offices and outside the local CBS television station WCCO, where Kroll's wife was a news anchor and reporter. They believed it was a conflict of interest for Kroll's wife to cover the MPD. Armstrong had even tried to put pressure on the mayor to uproot Kroll. She eventually helped organize a demonstration outside Kroll's home in the northern suburb of Hugo, Minnesota. A large crowd, many wearing T-shirts that read "Bob KKKroll Must Go," gathered outside Kroll's house to demand that he be fired.

To Armstrong and others in the community, Kroll represented the old guard of the Minneapolis Police Department—the old guard being those who beat people up and asked questions later. She knew it was ingrained in the department's culture for some officers to behave badly and that a lack of accountability allowed their hostility to fester. "Kroll's presence and his public statements after police killings contributed to a hostile atmosphere for communities of color and those protesting police violence," Nekima Levy Armstrong said in remarks to the ACLU. "He should have been held accountable a long time ago."

Her persistence, and the expert legal teams at the ACLU and Fish and Richardson, finally yielded results on April 4, 2023. That morning, I awoke to headlines proclaiming that Bob Kroll had been banned from serving as a police officer in Minneapolis or the surrounding counties for the next ten years. Nor could he serve in any capacity on the Minnesota Board of Peace Officer Standards and Training. Kroll had agreed to a settlement, and those were the terms.

Kroll told Alpha News, where his wife worked, that "MPD's failures have always been on police administration. The entire lawsuit was based on a concocted lie created by elected officials, representatives, and PR consultants in Minneapolis and the Capitol to blame Minneapolis's failures on me personally."

I had appealed to Kroll, had tried to persuade him to retire from the MPD, and he wouldn't budge. But unbeknownst to me, my unconventional allies had been working on a plan of their own. Armstrong's victory was the best kind of surprise. It felt like poetic justice to me. "We were thrilled when we signed the settlement agreement that included those provisions," Armstrong later told me. "It was a team effort and it worked. We see the fruit of that, when you don't have someone emboldening officers to do some of the harm they were doing."

In my thirty-plus years in the profession, I have never heard of citizens coming together through litigation to oust the head of a police union and ban him from wearing the uniform for the next decade. Kroll had been up against powerful attorneys and plaintiffs who refused to give up. The people grant the police their power, and they took it back. I can only imagine how Kroll feels about that. I hope he finally realizes that the problem with being a strongman is that there will always be someone stronger than you.

14

A Drawing on a Napkin

I STOOD BEFORE THE MINNEAPOLIS CITY COUNCIL IN JULY 2019 AND DIRECTED THEIR attention to a single point of data so unsettling that I felt certain my audience could not ignore it. On my PowerPoint slide, highlighted in red, was the number 1,251. That was the number of Minneapolis residents who had called 911 in the previous twelve months only to be told there were no squads available to send. These 1,251 citizens had experienced assaults, domestic violence, shootings, burglaries in progress, overdoses, and other life-threatening situations. Their calls were designated "priority one."

Imagine you are asleep in an upstairs bedroom in your home, your children are sleeping down the hall, and you hear the sound of breaking glass from below. You hear footsteps where none should be. Someone has broken into your home. You call 911. And instead of telling you "the police are on their way," the dispatcher says, "We'll get to you as soon as we can." How many minutes will it take that unknown prowler to ascend the stairs? What will you do if that happens? You've always believed there is a safety net you can depend on. But on the night danger enters your home, that safety net has a hole in it. You're on your own. This waking nightmare terrorized 1,251 citizens of our city between July 2018 and July 2019. The backup of "pending" calls was the result of understaffing in the MPD. Each pending call had the potential to endanger citizens, impede criminal investigations, and erode public trust. Surely, I thought, if the city council members and I could agree on anything, it would be that calling 911 should not be a roll of the dice. As it turned out, I was wrong.

I had come before the city council that day to present information in advance of the city's annual budget meeting. In November, I would plead with the council to hire four hundred officers by 2025. That was the long-term goal—the number calculated to meet the needs of the city's growing population, respond to emergencies, and maintain crime-prevention strategies while supporting the health and well-being of MPD officers. The immediate, urgent need was for thirty officers—and even with that, we would not break even. Each year, the MPD loses forty officers to normal attrition.

I did the best I could to advocate on behalf of the people of Minneapolis—and to appeal to the council members, regardless of their political beliefs. All my requests were evidence-based. In addition to the backlogged 911 calls, I was concerned about the health and well-being of my officers who were stressed and worn down from working excessive overtime because we were understaffed. We ought to care about the people who are putting themselves in harm's way to keep us safe; it's the right thing to do, and it benefits everyone. Fatigued officers generate more complaints from civilians. Internal Affairs complaints rise when officers are overworked and overstressed. Perhaps it seemed counterintuitive to some council members that to reduce excessive force, more police are needed, not fewer. But they weren't going to take a moment to look up from their preconceptions, survey the landscape, and call on their own common sense and reason.

The data also show that more community-connected officers walking on foot in our neighborhoods is likely to deter crime and reduce the number of arrests—helping to disrupt the "prison pipeline" that disproportionately impacts people of color. I used to be a beat officer, and I know that relationships are based on proximity. To build trust with the community, we need to be available to them. But by the time I stood before the city council in 2019, I had been forced to eliminate all foot beats. The MPD had so few patrol officers that all I could do was send them racing around in squad cars from call to call. They didn't have time to do proactive policing to address ongoing issues in the neighborhoods. Our investigators were also stretched so thin they could barely keep up with the surge of cases arising from gun violence and the devastating opioid epidemic. I firmly believed we should have had a sworn staff of twelve hundred officers in 2019, based on calls for service, staffing up footbeats and investigators, and staying above normal attrition losses. By that measure, we were already at a deficit of at least two hundred officers.

My plea to the city council in 2019 turned out to be prescient. Back then, we were already unable to respond adequately to the 911 calls that occurred daily in a big city. I warned the council: If a large-scale emergency should occur, the floodgates would not hold. With sufficient MPD staffing, the next crisis could be managed; without it, we were on a collision course with catastrophe. A year before George Floyd was murdered, our city was already living on borrowed time. I knew that at some point, the city's luck was going to run out.

In October 2019, a month before the city council's budget hearings, Police Federation president Bob Kroll spoke from the podium at a campaign rally for Donald Trump. Dressed in his bright red "Cops for Trump" T-shirt, Kroll bitterly accused the Obama administration of "handcuffing and oppressing" the police. He soaked up the applause when he extolled Trump for "letting the cops do their jobs" and for "putting the handcuffs on the criminals instead of us." Kroll's mocking, mustachioed grin beamed forth from local and national newscasts as he needled the rally crowd to sit down and debate the facts with the left. "And when their facts don't hold up," Kroll said, "wait to be labeled a racist."

A few weeks after Kroll's grandstanding at the Trump rally, I walked into the chambers of one the most left-leaning and progressive city councils in the country to advocate for hiring more police officers. If I had any hope of success, it lay in believing that reasonable people would be able to bypass the theater and the politics and take in the facts. That hope vanished when I looked around the council chamber and saw about a dozen color printouts of a photo from the rally. The photos showed Bob Kroll posing with Donald Trump. Community members had taped the photos to the dais where the council members sat—and the council made no effort to remove them.

There were moments during my tenure as chief when it seemed like all the adults had left the building. Nowhere was this more evident than the city council chamber that day. The council had chosen to signal their intentions before I had the chance to speak. I knew that all I could do at that point was enter my remarks into the public record. I was unemotional when I delivered my budget presentation. I wasn't trying to instill fear. I proposed solutions based on research. I outlined a realistic timeline to build up the MPD's staffing, starting with the thirty officers I urgently needed that year. In the end, the city council granted the funds to hire fourteen officers. With attrition, I would enter 2020 with about twenty-five fewer officers than the year before, and two hundred less than the data indicated were necessary.

The opposing ideologies of Kroll and the council had reached a stalemate that my data had no power to referee. And both sides were responsible for the impasse. When Kroll, as union president, chose to take to the national stage as a hard-line obstructionist to police reform, he had to know that would not benefit the department's budget negotiations. Was Kroll looking out for the rank and file that he supposedly represented? At the time I made my staffing appeal to the council, the mid-shift officers in the 1st Precinct had been held over 262 times in the past six months, which meant that officers could not go home at the end of their shifts because there were not enough resources to handle the incoming calls for service. Who benefited when Kroll undermined my efforts to relieve the overworked patrol officers?

At the same time, it's hard for me to believe that the council members had the best interests of the city's 911 callers in mind. I believe displaying the Kroll photos in council chambers was not only a snub, but also an act of misdirection. I have observed that there are times when people with an agenda need a monster. The council found one in Kroll. They knew he was doing real damage, yet they needed him because he was a useful foil to help elevate their own message. Just like Kroll, the council members were playing to the cameras and to their base. They were using their power of the purse punitively, but it was the people in their wards who would suffer.

The city council's disinvestment in the MPD pushed me to look elsewhere for support. Over the next two years, I sought and obtained Federal and foundation grants to fill critical gaps in funding. But even when I brought free money to the table, the council turned it down. In March 2020—prior to George Floyd's murder—reconstruction of I-35 W in Minneapolis had been under-way for a couple of years, and people were using the neighborhood streets as secondary arteries, creating speeding hazards and resulting in car accidents in residential neighborhoods. Areas with the largest populations of people of color were experiencing the highest rates of injuries to drivers and pedestrians. I had the opportunity to apply for a $1.3 million Federal grant to fund an additional ten traffic offi-cers to focus on public safety and traffic enforcement in the affected communities. At the time, our traffic unit had dwindled to just four traffic investigators, who were responding to crashes involving death or serious injuries, but lacked the bandwidth to assist in the neigh-borhoods. I am well aware of the sensitivities around racial profiling in traffic stops. But I also listened to Black leaders and community members who supported additional traffic enforcement because, simply put, people were getting run over in the streets. Nevertheless, council member Steven Fletcher introduced a measure to prohibit me from applying for the grant. Fletcher's stated reason, despite my repeated warnings of the consequences of understaffing, was that the additional traffic investigators might "unnecessarily" grow the police department.

Six months later, the Department of Justice (DOJ) offered the Minneapolis Police Department a competitive, $3 million Federal grant aimed at reducing excessive force. The funds were part of a new national initiative that would launch in Minneapolis. DOJ representatives came to the city to meet with business and commu-nity leaders, including our Black elders, activists, faith leaders, and educators. These community members expressed that they needed police officers—but they needed good police officers. This grant would have funded key components of my plan to improve the MPD, including retraining, policy reform, and wellness support. But the council rejected it.

The Minneapolis City Council would not invest in the MPD's future even if they were given free money to do so. They wanted to burn the house down. Two weeks after the murder of George Floyd, nine city council members held a rally in Powderhorn Park. They stood onstage behind a giant banner that read "DEFUND THE POLICE" and announced their intention to dismantle the MPD. The group of nine held a veto-proof majority on the council.

We were at the most critical juncture in our state's history in terms of public safety. The city was on fire and the whole world was watching, yet we couldn't get even one news feed of all thirteen city council members locked arm in arm to say that we needed peace in our city. I should not have been able to turn on the news in the morning or at night without hearing from our elected council members that we were going to get accountability for George Floyd's murder, but that we needed peace and we needed everyone to come together. It was the largest, most significant crisis on their watch, as it was on mine. Where were these nine council members when we needed them to say: "Do not create more trauma to our communities?" Evidently they were planning to make a move that would introduce further uncertainty. The Powderhorn Park announcement suited their agenda, but it did nothing to address the city's most urgent needs.

The majority of council members on that Powderhorn Park stage who wanted to defund the MPD didn't look like me. They might be able to just get up and move to another neighborhood, or they might be fortunate to live in a section of Minneapolis that didn't have a need for constant 911 calls—but what about the people who were directly experiencing the impact of rising crime? What if you were someone who didn't have the opportunity to freely move? The city's Black leaders spoke up for the community most affected by both police violence and community violence, and many opposed the referendum. Nekima Levy Armstrong had always called out police misconduct and fought for reform, and I didn't know where she would stand on the issue until I read the op-ed she wrote for the *Minneapolis Star Tribune*. Armstrong held the city council accountable, too. "Those of us who had long fought for a reckoning over police abuse in Minneapolis expected . . . a well-thought-out, evidence-based, comprehensive plan to remake our police department," she wrote. "Instead, what we got was progressive posturing of a kind seen throughout the country and a missed opportunity to bring about real change and racial justice."

When pressed for a concrete description of what the city's future would look like with less police funding, perhaps some of the council members began to have second thoughts. But it was too late. They were locked in. I was hoping that calmer heads would come to their senses and realize that the rally in the park was good theater, but bad governance. Instead, the council went on to propose an amendment to the city's charter to replace the police with a new organization: the Department of Community Safety and Violence Prevention. How this new organization would work and what it would do differently was a mystery, and would remain so. But one thing was clear: Swiftly and all at once, the MPD was canceled.

As the city was burning, I was trying to keep our population safe. At the same time, major institutions began to announce that they were not going to engage with the MPD to have a public safety presence anymore. On May 28, the University of Minnesota issued a statement that it would no longer contract with the MPD for security at games and other large events. Nobody from the university contacted me to discuss their change of heart—I heard about it on the news, on the same day that the 3rd Precinct was destroyed. On June 3, the Minneapolis Public Schools eliminated school resource officers. We were still living with the memories of Columbine and Parkdale. Active shooter drills were a regular part of students' routines. But now the district had decided to remove an armed, plainclothes school resource officer as a first line of defense. Instead, the Minneapolis Public Schools would rely upon unarmed staff.

Some longtime allies will withdraw their support during a crisis. That happens. But I had to stay focused. I centered myself: *Our children are watching us right now.* And I believed we were going to get through this. To keep the remaining threads of safety in our city from fraying, I had to draw upon the goodwill I had earned. I soon received a call from the Minnesota Twins' security director requesting a meeting. He wanted to discuss the team's arrangement with the MPD to provide security at games. I soon found myself observing the meticulously maintained Kentucky bluegrass of the Twins outfield from the vantage point of a private box at Target Field. About ten members of the Twins organization were in attendance, including Executive Chair Jim Pohlad, whose family had owned the team since 1984. I brought along officers Charles Adams Jr. and Steve Sporny.

The conversation started out somber. Mr. Pohlad and other executives shared that George Floyd's murder had deeply impacted their players, families, and employees. What seemed to weigh most on Mr. Pohlad's mind was the well-being of the Twins' diverse fan base. When fans enter the stadium and the first people they see are wearing a uniform now viewed by many with distrust, would they feel safe and respected? Mr. Pohlad was listening to the concerns of staff members who lived in Minneapolis and were people of color, and was mindful of the players and their personal experiences with racial profiling.

"Chief," said Mr. Pohlad, "why should we continue to employ your officers here at the stadium?"

He looked me in the eye when he spoke. I could tell he would give my answer the full weight of his consideration.

I explained to Mr. Pohlad why I fired Chauvin and the other officers. I talked about procedural justice. I reminded the group of my steadfast vision and plan to change MPD culture. Now more than ever, I said, our communities need to see the city's major organizations walk and chew gum at the same time. I said that two things can be true at once. The Minneapolis Police Department needs reform, and we still need a police department to keep us safe. I also wanted to share how sports has played a role in building the relationship between the MPD and our communities. I said, "Before you make a decision, I would like for you to hear from these two officers who are volunteer coaches and have probably run drills with some of the young fans who come to Twins games. I want you to understand where their hearts are at and why they do this job."

Officers Adams and Sporny denounced what Derek Chauvin had done. They shared how painful it was that someone who wore the same uniform had taken a life and triggered the tension and violence in the city. Adams and Sporny had built their careers around forging positive relationships with the people they served. Adams had grown up in the city and was a volunteer coach of the Minneapolis North High School football team. He spoke about how sports had been a bridge for him to connect with young people in the precinct where he worked. Sporny spoke about how his many years of coaching youth sports was part of a life of service. Although not all kids can become a Major League Baseball player, he said, coaches and police officers can help instill in young people a notion of looking out for others and working hard to achieve their dreams.

A few days later, I heard back from the Twins' management. They had decided to continue the team's relationship with the MPD, but there was a condition: All the officers who had been working at the stadium had to reapply. I said, "Absolutely!" And I thanked them. The Twins were the Pohlad family's organization and the team means a lot to the people of Minnesota. I believe that by having officers reapply for their security jobs, Mr. Pohlad wanted to remind them that interacting with Twins fans was a privilege they needed to earn.

That season, the Twins home opener was the first professional sports event in Minneapolis since the COVID-19 pandemic started. There was still no vaccine, and gathering in large crowds was not yet permitted. When the players stood along the baselines for the national anthem, they removed their hats and stared out at thousands of empty seats. In this surreal setting, hope was present in the form of the great Minneapolis vocal ensemble Sounds of Blackness, who performed "Lift Every Voice and Sing." In the background, painted on the outfield wall, was a memorial to George Floyd. The Twins organization had found a way to communicate their stand on the death of George Floyd. They had also done their due diligence to prepare for the safety of their fans on the day in the near future when they could return to Target Field.

As more organizations began to question their security contracts with the MPD, I embarked on what I called a "table the emotion" tour. I met with other critical stakeholders in the city to remind them that, like myself, they have an obligation to keep their patrons, customers, and employees safe. I first appealed to their consciences and if that didn't break through, I focused on the bottom line. Big brands and business leaders understood that tragedy doesn't come cheap. Mass shootings around the country did not pause after May 25, 2020. Which one of these executives wanted to be at the podium during the press conference if a shooting occurred here? Who would like to explain to grieving family members that they felt it was in their best interests to not have armed officers in their facilities as a first line of defense?

I was thankful to the Twins and the other teams who were willing to give me the benefit of the doubt. The Minnesota Vikings also reached out to me, and I met with executives and players who were members of the team's social justice committee. I spoke to the leadership of the Minnesota Timberwolves. In the end, both organizations chose to maintain a relationship with the MPD. When I spoke to the coach and players of the Minnesota Lynx, they brought up specific concerns about Lt. Bob Kroll—and with good reason. In 2016, following the shooting of Philando Castile by police officers in a nearby suburb, Lynx players publicly denounced racial profiling. During a pregame warm-up at Target Center in Minneapolis, some players wore T-shirts that said "Black Lives Matter" and "Change Starts with Us." In response, four off-duty MPD officers who were working the game walked off the job. Bob Kroll championed the officers and their actions. Asked by a Minneapolis *Star Tribune* reporter if other officers would fill in for those who quit, Kroll replied, "If [the players] are going to keep their stance, all officers may refuse to work there." In typical fashion, Kroll chose to escalate the disagreement and claimed to speak for all MPD officers.

In the end, the Minnesota Lynx continued to work with the MPD. My meeting with them was not the first time Kroll's name had come up unfavorably in my conversations with civic, sports, and business leaders. Kroll was creating a self-fulfilling prophecy. His constant refrain was: Nobody understands us; they don't want us. And he was making those words come true. As chief, I was held to a higher standard. I didn't want to say anything that would give Kroll a twenty-second sound bite to feed his propaganda and lead even more officers off the cliff. I could not have a public fight with him, only direct and private conversations. In my meetings with city stakeholders, I continued to remind them that while Kroll was the union president, he wasn't the chief and these weren't his officers.

It wasn't long before the upheaval and economic losses of the summer of 2020 put the city's credit rating at risk. The city lost lucrative contracts when businesses decided not to move their employees from a suburb into downtown Minneapolis. Previously scheduled conventions signaled their plans to cancel events in Minneapolis. I stepped in to assist our city's Convention and Visitors Bureau team by filming public service announcements, assuring visitors their safety was not forgotten. Although participating in PSAs may seem far outside my lane as police chief, I was looking at the big picture. Disrupting the economic engine that keeps our hospitality workers receiving paychecks, restaurant reservations full, and Uber and Lyft drivers busy also disrupts a key part of our public safety ecosystem. I was doing everything I could to prevent conditions in our city going from bad to worse.

But the city council was determinedly pushing in the opposite direction. The council's ballot referendum would go before voters in the November 2021 election. The measure would remove the minimum staffing levels for sworn officers currently required by the city charter and enable the council to reallocate funds from police staffing to other city services, such as social workers and crisis managers. But there was no plan that detailed how these alternate services would meet public safety needs or respond to calls. The referendum did allow that "peace officers" could be a part of the new system, "if necessary." But the Minneapolis Police Department as we knew it would be replaced with a Department of Public Safety, and the oversight of this new agency would shift from the mayor's office to the city council.

Leading up to election day, I was hoping that reasonable minds would weigh in and really talk about how people would be impacted by the ballot referendum, if it passed. The new system would take effect within thirty days of the election. Yet there was no solid plan for implementation and no explanation of the mechanics of this new Department of Public Safety. As I said at the time, I was not expecting some kind of robust, detailed plan. But as the election drew closer, frankly, I would have taken a drawing on a napkin—and I had not seen that either.

I waited and waited, but nobody else stepped into this vacuum of common sense. I was certain that if the referendum passed, our city would once again find itself descending into chaos. I don't think the council members truly measured what this upheaval—in a community already reeling from trauma and uncertainty—could do to our city. As the days marched on toward November, a voice inside was telling me: You have to say "something."

I decided to hold a press conference.

I thought about my role and responsibility as the chief law enforcement officer for the city. What was missing from the public dialogue was the perspective of anyone with law enforcement experience. I had not been consulted in any way when the ballot referendum was drafted. But I feared that my silence on the matter would imply my approval. I thought about how to navigate speaking out from the perspective of public safety, but I knew I was crossing into a gray area. This was a political issue, and I needed to be as apolitical as possible. That's why I could not have the mayor, or any other elected official, standing beside me at the podium. I had to speak to this on my own, in my own voice. I predicted the mayor would be livid when I held the press conference without his knowledge or approval, but I wasn't thinking about job security. In the end, I simply decided that if I didn't speak out, I would have difficulty living with myself. And so I spoke out.

In my public remarks, I pointed out that if this measure passed, it would not only affect me, but it also would shape the future of the MPD for years to come, well beyond my tenure as chief. I told the people that this referendum would not prevent tragic incidents between police and community members from ever occurring again. It would not suddenly reset the culture of a police department that has been in existence for 155 years. Nor would it help the city's efforts to recruit, hire, and retain police professionals who wanted to change the department's culture for the better. And the measure would not eliminate the disparities in violent crime that have been a public health crisis in our city for decades.

This ballot measure claimed to offer a public health–oriented solution to the overhaul of policing, but it didn't address the realities of the public health crisis in Minneapolis. As of 2021, MPD crime analysis showed that for every 187 Black residents in our city, one Black person has been shot. Four out of five victims of violent crime in this city are Black. This is indeed a crisis. However, a person wearing the MPD uniform is not the greatest threat to the lives of Black people in Minneapolis. None of our officers wake up in the morning wanting to take a life. A Black person in Minneapolis is 480 times more likely to be shot by another civilian than to be the victim of an officer-involved shooting.

A holistic approach to public safety does not require a drastic change to our city charter. As much as we need to address the mental health and addiction crises that also play into this cycle of violence, social workers and drug counselors cannot investigate shootings and drug crimes and arrest the perpetrators. As I said in my press conference that day, the future of public safety in our city requires all of us to see each other as necessary.

As soon as the press conference was over, city council president Lisa Bender slapped me with an ethics complaint. I didn't lose any sleep over it. Bender had been making nonsensical comments on national news, yet I was compelled to silence. Bender had just told a CNN reporter that if someone was breaking into her home, she would not dial 911 because calling the police "comes from a place of privilege." I simply could not have Lisa Bender be the loudest voice speaking out on public safety. I don't care if you live in Minneapolis or the Taj Mahal—if someone is breaking into your home, call the police.

Because my press conference aired live, Mayor Frey heard about it after the fact. He called me and said, "Chief, can you tell me about what just occurred?" I said, "Mayor, I just completed a press conference and I spoke directly as chief about this ballot measure. I felt compelled through my duty and oath of office to address the citizens of the city on what its impact could be. I apologize that I did not inform you. However, I needed this to be a message without the optics of politics attached." It's never good to catch your boss off guard and blindside him, but I had done just that. Mayor Frey subsequently issued me a letter of reprimand. And I fully accepted that discipline; everybody needs to be held accountable, including me. It was right for Frey to do that, and it never changed our relationship. There can be times in one's career when moral and ethical obligations converge and you have to act, and you have to accept the consequences.

On election day, the citizens of Minneapolis turned out in record numbers to vote. When the results came in, I was up in the command post because we had a civil unrest situation in the Uptown neighborhood. We were monitoring footage of the disturbance from the pole cameras in the area, but we had set aside one screen for the evening news. The results of the vote were unequivocal. By a wide margin, voters rejected the proposal to dismantle the MPD. Citywide, 56 percent of voters were opposed. I felt proud of our city. Minneapolitans spoke loud and clear. Many who had a history of negative relationships with the MPD showed up to vote. The Black community used their votes to say: We can and we must hold the MPD accountable when they engage in misconduct, but we also need them. By getting rid of the police department and not having a plan to address crime and public safety, we'd only be endangered and retraumatized.

I think the voters ultimately showed the council that two things can be true at the same time. The vote said: We need a police department *and* we need the officers who work there to be professional, unbiased, and trustworthy. At that point I think people also had city council fatigue and they were tired. All thirteen seats on the city council were also up for election that November. Five of the incumbents lost their seats, including Steven Fletcher. Lisa Bender did not run for reelection.

There were many times during my tenure as chief that I said to myself, "I wish all I had to do was deal with crime." But there is no police chief in America who has that luxury. In Minneapolis, one year before the ballot referendum, we had experienced one of our history's most shocking and tragic police encounters, followed by the most destruction our city ever faced due to civil unrest. It sparked demonstrations across America and the globe. I'd venture to say that, for a time, the MPD was the most-hated police department in the world. Certainly in America. And yet, even with that, some of the very same communities that had the least amount of trust in the police department overwhelmingly denounced that ballot referendum. Think about that. It is a reflection of the enormous responsibility police officers have toward those we serve.

15
Breaking the Blue Wall

NEARLY THIRTY YEARS AFTER I SURPRISED A YOUNG LAWYER NAMED KEITH ELLISON by defying the "blue wall" of silence, Ellison came to see me again. This time, though the case was not about a white officer who called my uncle the N-word, Ellison's request was the same: He called me to testify against another MPD officer. Ellison, by then, was the Minnesota attorney general and I was the chief of police. I was being called to speak the truth, again, so that we could bring justice for George Floyd. It was the fall of 2021 and Ellison was leading the prosecution of Derek Chauvin on charges of second-degree unintentional murder, third-degree murder, and second-degree manslaughter.

The previous year, Minnesota governor Tim Walz had reassigned the Chauvin case from the Hennepin County attorney to the Minnesota attorney general in response to concerns expressed by the public, the protesters, and George Floyd's family. Many worried that justice would not be served if the system they already distrusted was allowed to conduct its business as usual. I shared this concern.

Only 2 percent of killings by police, nationally, result in officers being charged with a crime. And while it's exceedingly rare for officers to be prosecuted, it's even more rare for them to be convicted.

I've seen enough to know that the platforms of justice can sometimes have holes in them. That's why my first move, after watching the bystander video of Floyd's death, was to try to plug those holes. By waking up FBI Special Agent in Charge Rainer Drolshagen the night of Floyd's murder, I had set in motion a Federally directed backup plan in case state authorities declined to prosecute. I felt reassured now that the state's case was being led by Minnesota's top law enforcement official with a team of top-tier attorneys. The state's case would be heard first, and the Federal trial would follow. I think Ellison and I both knew, professionally and in our hearts, the gravity of the case we were preparing for.

In Minneapolis, the anger, sadness, and frustration of 2020 had shifted to stress and uncertainty about Derek Chauvin's imminent trial. Would Chauvin's trial be a repeat of the outcome we had come to expect? Even with video evidence, police had been acquitted many times before—from the LAPD officers who beat Rodney King in 1992 to the officer acquitted for shooting Philando Castile in a Twin Cities suburb in 2017. Would Chauvin's trial reinforce the sense that, for people of color, justice is out of reach?

I've testified many times before and I have never seen a team of attorneys take such care in preparing for trial. The most minute detail was important to the prosecution team. They truly believed that due process matters, and they respected that, under our system of law, Chauvin was innocent until proven guilty. I never had the sense that they believed Darnella Frazier's video assured a conviction. The attorneys took the time to put together a thorough and painstaking case. Attorney Steven Schleicher worked with me to make sure I was prepared for my testimony. I had an idea of what defense attorney Eric Nelson was going to ask me, and that his questions would center on MPD training and policy—but he could ask me anything he wanted. I have the utmost respect for Eric Nelson for his vigorous defense of Chauvin. He stepped up for one of the toughest cases in recent history and did an admirable job.

Chauvin's trial would not be the first time I had testified in court against an MPD officer. I was assistant chief when Officer Mohamed Noor shot Justine Damond, and was appointed chief in the aftermath of the shooting. I fired Noor, and testified at his 2019 trial that there were no MPD policies or procedures that would ever justify Noor's shooting of Justine Damond. And beyond defying our policies, Noor's actions had also defied our training and professional ethics. Prior to the Noor case, I don't recall another instance in the modern history of the MPD that a chief of police took the stand at a criminal trial testifying against his own officer. Yet my willingness to give testimony in the Noor trial was not mirrored by others on the force. Dozens of officers refused to appear to give voluntary statements. Some had to be compelled by subpoenas to appear in court. Noor was initially convicted of third-degree murder and manslaughter, but the Minnesota Supreme Court overturned the murder conviction and his 12.5-year sentence. Noor wound up serving just over three years for manslaughter. This outcome underscored the uncertainties of verdicts that are subject to appeal.

Late in the morning of April 5, 2021, I got a call from Steve Schleicher who said, "Rondo, you're up. It looks like you're going to be called today. I'll see you in court." It was the eighth day of the Chauvin trial. The courthouse occupies one tower of the twenty-four-story Hennepin County Government Center in the middle of downtown Minneapolis. The security for the trial was the highest I'd ever seen in the city—and that's because there had been threats. The Government Center was surrounded by concrete barriers and razor wire fencing. Windows were boarded up. There were sweeps with bomb-sniffing dogs. The entire building was shut down for nearly all activity except the trial, but sections of the plaza outside remained open for peaceful protesters to gather. The jurors had escorts to and from the courtroom, and their addresses were protected. National Guard troops stood watch outside and kept a lookout from Humvees restricting access to the Government Center parking ramp entrance. Hennepin County Sheriff's Department personnel screened jurors, judges, attorneys, and witnesses before they entered the building.

I presented my ID, signed in, and checked my weapon. The bailiff escorted me into the courtroom and I approached the bench to be sworn in as a witness. I wore my full uniform. I removed my hat and stood facing Judge Peter Cahill, separated by a plexiglass screen and wearing a face mask. I raised my right hand and swore to tell the truth.

I took a seat in the witness box and saw attorney Steve Schleicher standing in front of me at the podium. During his opening questions, Schleicher asked me if I recognized the defendant, Derek Chauvin, and could identify him there in the courtroom that day. It was the first time that I ever recall seeing Derek Chauvin and being in the same room with him. I had never met him during my time in the department, and I'd never even worked in the same building with him. But like millions of people around the world, I recognized his face. I identified Chauvin and questioning began. It was a packed courtroom. A few reporters sat in the room, and I knew there was also an overflow room for journalists. But nobody would have to wait for the evening news to learn about the day's testimony. The entire trial was being broadcast live. For the first time in Minnesota, the judge had allowed cameras in the courtroom—due in part to the seating restrictions imposed by the COVID-19 pandemic but also because of the public interest in the trial. "I was convinced that if we did not televise that trial, the results, no matter which way it went, were never going to be accepted by the community," Judge Cahill later told Minnesota Public Radio.

Even though I was the police chief for Minneapolis, I knew that every word I spoke would be perceived as representative of the American policing system. Not only Derek Chauvin but also the profession of policing was on trial that day. I felt the weight and immensity of my responsibility. The most important thing for me to do was to express my humanity and my values. I was very intentional about appearing in my chief's uniform. It was highly unusual for a police chief to testify against a former officer in such a high-profile trial. American juries had rarely, if ever, seen that before. I wanted to show the world that police chiefs must be the ones to call out misconduct within our profession. We can't look the other way, and we can't rely on community members to point out misconduct for us.

My testimony for the prosecution was groundbreaking in the sense that, for hundreds of years, police departments took care of their dirty laundry in-house. As chief, I am the only one who can give discipline. So I terminated Chauvin and the other officers immediately, without requiring an investigation. I had made up my mind to fire them when I saw Darnella Frazier's video. Terminating those officers was within my purview as chief of police. As their employer, that was my lane. But for many years, in many cities, police chiefs would have gone no further than that. Chiefs could fire a problem officer and tell themselves they'd done their part. But it's one thing to hold an officer accountable in an employment matter because you are their boss, and quite another to bear witness against that officer in a criminal proceeding. Some chiefs would question why they should publicly expose something tragic, or corrupt, that happened within their organization when they could simply stick to their lane and let any criminal charges play out on their own. If chiefs testify against one of their own at trial, they don't get to go into witness protection afterward like a mafia informer in a movie. They have to return to their job. And when they do, they may very well find themselves on the outside of the insular culture of policing.

But a chief must be willing to go the distance. Those who wear this uniform must hold each other accountable. Anything less is hypocritical. Police departments expect and demand that community members speak out on gun violence, drug dealing, and other crimes in their neighborhoods. We expect bystanders and even family members to testify as witnesses in criminal court all the time. If there's any hope of police being viewed as legitimate, we need to do everything we're telling community members to do. If we are truly committed to addressing and fixing a problem, we must speak out on it. Police chiefs must be held to the highest standard, not the minimum requirements. As a leader I am duty bound to uphold my values and principles. On May 25, 2020, one of my officers killed an unarmed man in broad daylight. I feel horrible that a life was taken on my watch. But I didn't run from that. I put on my uniform and I took the stand.

I testified that it was my firm belief that the one singular incident a police officer will be judged on forever will be their use of force. And so, while it was absolutely imperative that our officers go home at the end of their shifts, we wanted to make sure that our community members go home, too. This imperative is encoded in our use-of-force policy, which stated that the sanctity of life and the protection of the public shall be the priority in any interaction. Police were not permitted to use force without limits or without discretion. Rather, any use of force must be reasonable and appropriate to the situation.

When questioned about what I saw on the bystander video, I acknowledged that there was an initial reasonableness in trying to get Mr. Floyd under control in the first few seconds of the encounter. But once there was no longer any resistance, and clearly when Mr. Floyd was no longer responsive and even motionless, to continue to apply that level of force to a person proned out, and handcuffed behind his back—that in no way, shape, or form is permitted by MPD policy. I stated unequivocally that Chauvin's sustained and unnecessary use of force against George Floyd was not part of our training, and was certainly not part of our ethics or our values.

I testified that police officers are called to serve with compassion and without bias. To serve with compassion means we see each other as necessary, we value each other, and we treat all people with the dignity and respect they deserve. Chauvin was not making a split-second decision in a situation where lives were at stake. He had nine minutes and twenty-nine seconds to consider his actions. Bystanders were begging him to stop, George Floyd was pleading for his life, and one of the other officers at the scene even suggested they place Mr. Floyd in a recovery position. Chauvin defied a principle that has been central to policing throughout the history of the profession: in our custody, in our care. We have a duty to render aid to any person in our custody who is in distress. This duty derives from our highest principle: to respect and value human life.

Policing is a job that requires its people to care. Our humanity showed up that day in the form of seven other MPD officers who also came forward to speak the truth. Lt. Richard Zimmerman, Inspector Katie Blackwell, Sgt. David Pleoger, Sgt. Jon Edwards, Sgt. Ker Yang, Lt. Johnny Mercil, and Officer Nicole Mackenzie also testified for the prosecution. This was something else that Americans had rarely seen before. Not only did the police chief testify, but he was not a lone wolf or an isolated whistleblower. Lt. Zimmerman and Inspector Blackwell delivered particularly compelling testimony that Chauvin's actions could not be justified by departmental training or policy. Lt. Zimmerman, the longest-tenured employee of the MPD with more than thirty-five years on the force at the time of the trial, was the head of homicide. He stated, "First of all pulling [Floyd] down to the ground face down and putting your knee on a neck for that amount of time is just uncalled for. I saw no reason why the officers felt they were in danger."

I believe the officers who testified have a hardwired values-based and ethics-based spirit. This type of person is the most significant contributor to changing culture. Why? Because it's clear that they're not thinking about any consequences or backlash from a deep-rooted, broken system or toxic culture. They don't have the same fear that others do—even though such systems have a history of punishing those who don't fall in line.

What happened at Thirty-Eighth and Chicago not only shocked the conscience but also ripped a hole in the heart of this profession. I believe Chauvin's inhumanity was a rallying cry for those who took pride in being a guardian of the people and they said: "No way. I can't stay silent on this." From the officers across the country who lined up and took a knee to the group of us who testified in the Hennepin County courthouse, cracks were forming in the "blue wall" that has long protected officers from accountability.

For many weeks before the trial, I had been out speaking with community stakeholders. I briefed business owners and community leaders on the city's security plan, which included a National Guard presence throughout the trial. I met with the ACLU to talk about how street closures and other measures would impact the unsheltered and how the MPD was working with our social services street outreach teams to take care of them. I was regularly on the phone with an interfaith group of Christian, Muslim, and Jewish faith leaders. I wanted to make clear to all stakeholders how they and their communities would be treated and what they could expect during the trial and after the verdict.

I also needed them. I said, if you're hearing things out in your community that are a concern, I need to know. Especially if there's a threat. For example, I had received information about armed men driving around South Minneapolis in pickup trucks with darkened license plates. I was trying to determine the temperature of the city—where are people feeling comfortable, and where are they feeling uneasy?

Almost everyone I met expressed anxiety. South Side residents were acutely aware of the ruins and rubble remaining on Lake Street nearly a year after the worst of the civil unrest had passed. These remnants of destruction were a constant visual reminder of despair and they fueled concerns about what the aftermath of a verdict would do to a city that had just begun to recover. I was hearing that people wanted accountability but understood that, in and of itself, a guilty verdict was not going to rebuild the city. Most of all, they feared the psychological trauma that a not-guilty verdict could cause. The people of Minneapolis are capable and resilient, but there is only so much a community can take. The small businesses were reopening, the big corporate stores were rebuilding, children were returning to classrooms in person. But if another trigger caused repeated violence, damage, and destruction, would that push our city past the point of recovery?

As concerned as I was for our city, I was equally concerned for the members of our department. We already had experienced the most unprecedented civil unrest in our state's history the previous summer. We were still dealing with the fallout from that. Crime was high, but MPD staffing was the lowest it had ever been. In the past year we had lost a third of our officers. Some had quit or retired, some had taken PTSD claims. We had gone from dangerously understaffed to catastrophically understaffed. And yet, for those officers who continued to show up and do their jobs, threats did not stop. Dispatchers were still receiving fake 911 calls that were traps. And I worried, when would our luck run out?

By this time, the division in our nation had built up to a crescendo. In the national dialogue, the BLM movement had entered into the social conversation and was countered with the rhetoric of "blue lives matter." Black Lives Matter signs appeared on lawns and so did "thin blue line" images that resembled an American flag but with a blue stripe. Several police departments nationally had banned police displays of the "thin blue line" flag because the imagery had morphed from a symbol of support for police to a symbol of far-right and white supremacist ideology. Federal authorities had received intelligence that there were bad actors, with white supremacist and extremist leanings, who had been in town or would be in town. The us-against-them mentality had become more entrenched and more palpable. Now there was a drumbeat: BLM, thin blue line, you don't respect Black lives, you don't respect blue lives. And I was trying to make sure that our officers continue to tune out this drumbeat and remember: The only thing that matters is the oath we took.

Every day of the trial, our multi-agency team had been meeting in the command post, assessing security concerns and evaluating threats. After three weeks of testimony, the jury started their deliberation. We didn't know if the verdict would be announced in two hours or two weeks. But we had been planning and preparing for months. I reported to the command post along with General Shawn Manke of the National Guard and representatives of the FBI, State

Patrol, and the Hennepin County Sheriff's office. I was regularly briefing the mayor. The MPD and National Guard teams were in place at strategic locations in the city. Many safety measures had already been enacted. Minneapolis Public Schools had shifted to remote learning, and most downtown businesses had their employees working remotely. Governor Walz announced a curfew for the three metro counties.

We had a television on in the command post, and were watching along with the rest of the world to hear what the verdict would be. I fielded calls from peers across the country who were also bracing for the news. Some states were putting their National Guard units on standby. All the major city police chiefs were extending resources to deal with whatever would happen next. When I talked to LA Chief Mike Moore, the entire LAPD was in uniform. Elsewhere in Minneapolis, thousands of people gathered on the plaza outside the courthouse and at the intersection of Thirty-Eighth and Chicago, which had become known as George Floyd Square.

I remember when we got word in the command post that the verdict was imminent. The command staff representing all the different agencies let their leaders in the field know, "It's coming. Everybody on post. This is what we planned for." I texted my counterparts across the country and messaged community stakeholders to get ready. Seated around a conference table in the command post, I looked up at the TV and saw the people in the courtroom rise as the jury entered. The jurors had deliberated for ten hours, over two days. "Members of the jury," said Judge Cahill, "I understand you have a verdict." Judge Cahill opened an envelope containing the jury's findings. As he read the first count, all of us in the command post were still and silent, listening for his words. On television, Derek Chauvin stood before the judge and jury, eyes darting back and forth above his mask. "We the jury in the above entitled matter as to count one, unintentional second-degree murder while committing a felony, find the defendant guilty," read Judge Cahill. Not a word was uttered in the command post as the second count was read: guilty. And the third count: guilty.

The room at the Hennepin County Government Center reserved for George Floyd's family erupted in tears and cheers. Shouts of joy, triumph, and relief rose from the plaza outside and from George Floyd Square. Strangers hugged each other and cried at the news that Chauvin had been found guilty on all three counts. This scene was repeated all across the world, but inside the command post, there was no emotional reaction at all.

I am sure that everyone in the command post experienced intense feelings as the verdict was read. But we were on the job, we were wearing our uniforms, and our focus needed to remain on keeping our community safe. And that's how it should be. Every single leader in that command room took an oath to the Constitution and that meant we had to respect the court's ruling regardless of what our personal feelings were. We were respecting the democratic process and the decision of those twelve jurors.

It's not a perfect system. We all know that. But I was proud of how it worked that time, because of the diligence of everyone involved. My sense was that if the verdict had been "not guilty," millions of people around the world would have had serious doubts about the integrity of the American justice system. Justice is supposed to be blind—but the people are not. They saw with their own eyes what Derek Chauvin did to George Floyd. A verdict of not guilty would have been in stark contradiction to what millions had plainly seen. I respect the jury's verdict and the discretion used by Judge Peter Cahill, who sentenced Derek Chauvin to 22.5 years in prison. As Americans, we should find hope in that process.

A single verdict does not erase history, and the past is filled with examples of officers in Minneapolis and across the country who have never been held accountable for misconduct or mistreatment or murder. But moving forward, no one could ever say that the people and the police of Minneapolis have never held their officers accountable in the criminal justice system. It came at great cost, but it happened. We can't say that Minneapolis police officers would never go against the blue wall of silence to publicly condemn the wrongdoing of one of their own. We hope that such a tragedy never happens again. But when it does, it cannot be said that no chief in America has ever testified against his own officer. For all the chiefs to come, this should be a turning point. It set new expectations for them to carry forward. This measure of justice for George Floyd is part of our history now, and our future should be brighter if we learn from it.

Rainer Drolshagen also came through on the promise he made to me the night of George Floyd's murder. Drolshagen's FBI investigation resulted in Federal civil rights charges that carried a stiff penalty. In December of that year, Chauvin pleaded guilty to the Federal charges, admitting to "willfully depriving, while acting under color of law, George Floyd of his constitutional rights, resulting in Mr. Floyd's bodily injury and death." Chauvin was sentenced to twenty-one years in Federal prison, to be served concurrently with his state sentence. I was relieved that the Federal conviction was in place when Chauvin appealed his state sentence, as he had the right to do. In the end, his state appeal was rejected.

Like many in Minneapolis, I felt that Chauvin's state and Federal convictions delivered a sense of justice for George Floyd. I also knew that much more work needed to be done—work from a justice standpoint and also work for our city to heal and repair. Chauvin would answer for his crimes, and so would the three officers who failed to stop him. The Minneapolis Police Department had in its policy—before May 25, 2020—a duty to intervene. All officers have a moral, ethical, and in some cases a legal duty to intervene to prevent another officer from harming someone. This policy, which remains in effect today, has *never* been based on an officer's years of service. This policy applies equally from the chief down to the most recently hired recruit. For those who believe a new recruit on their FTO training should get a pass because of the difficulty of speaking out against a senior officer—out of fear of reprisal and not passing their FTO program—I would simply ask: If you are the person being harmed and your rights violated, does it feel better knowing this is being done to you by a newer officer as opposed to a senior officer?

By their failure to act, Thomas Lane, J. Alexander Kueng, and Tou Thao were complicit in the murder of George Floyd. On February 24, 2022, following a trial that lasted more than a month, a Federal jury convicted all three officers of the same criminal civil rights violations that Chauvin had previously pleaded guilty to. Each received a Federal prison sentence: Thao for 42 months, Kueng for 36 months, and Lane for 30 months. The officers had failed in their duty to intervene and later that year were tried and convicted on state charges of aiding and abetting second-degree manslaughter. Kueng pleaded guilty and was sentenced to 3.5 years in prison. Lane pleaded guilty and was sentenced to 3 years. Thao was sentenced to 4 years and 9 months. Their state sentences were to be served concurrently with their Federal sentences.

Just a year after Chauvin, Kueng, Lane, and Thao received their final sentences, I watched another horrific video—this time from Memphis. Tyre Nichols, a twenty-nine-year-old Black man, was brutally assaulted by five officers. Many other officers looked on and did nothing. Paramedics were walking by him as he succumbed to his injuries on the side of the road. He died in the hospital three days later.

Every one of those people had an obligation to render him aid and care. When I watched the video of Nichols's tragic killing, I thought: How is this possible? But it happened. So the work continues.

Days after the tragic death of Mr. Tyre Nichols and prior to the release of the video to the public, I received a call from Memphis police chief C. J. Davis, who was the city's first Black female chief. I didn't have a playbook for what happened in the spring and summer of 2020—but I left a playbook for others to follow. This playbook was born of necessity and assembled on the fly. But because of what happened in Minneapolis, Chief Davis knew that the atrocity in her city could not be swept aside or explained away. Because of what we learned in Minneapolis, the people of Memphis didn't have to experience the worst of what we went through in terms of violent civil unrest. Chief Davis had time to respond to Nichols's killing and she did some things right. She immediately fired the officers. She did not try to defend their actions. The Memphis City Council came together with the Nichols family and said they were going to get justice, but they needed peace. As I write this book, two of the former officers pleaded guilty to Federal charges. Three other former officers were acquitted of the most severe charges they faced, but were convicted on lesser charges.

I've often said that there are four steps needed for change to occur. First, dream it. Envision the change you want to achieve. Second, the struggle. This is the most important part. I have chronicled many struggles in this book, from the brave stand taken by Arthur and Edith Lee to the determination of Nekima Levy Armstrong to "put the fire" wherever there is smoke. I have faced my own struggles throughout my life and career. This is the most critical aspect of creating change, because change doesn't come easy. The third step is victory: You achieve the change you seek. The fourth step: Begin again.

16

Minneapolis Will
Never Be the Same

BEFORE DAWN ON A CALM JUNE NIGHT IN 2021, I SAT ALONE IN MY CAR NEXT TO
Phelps Park—the setting of so many childhood memories—and
spoke into a toy walkie-talkie. The pint-sized plastic device worked
surprisingly well, given that I was communicating over a full city
block to the corner of Thirty-Eighth and Chicago. The time had
come to remove the concrete barriers that had surrounded George
Floyd Square for more than a year—roadblocks that prevented cars,
fire trucks, ambulances, snowplows, and city sanitation vehicles from
entering the area.

But some groups in the city were hell bent on preventing the
reopening of the intersection to traffic. If they got wind of our plans
over the police scanner, we would have a conflict on our hands.
So we found a solution in the Target toy aisle, and equipped our
team of city workers and community volunteers with the simple
walkie-talkies.

This operation had been a long time coming. Too long, in my
opinion. Over the previous year, the six-block radius surrounding

George Floyd Square had been overrun with crime—and rats. These were the inevitable consequences of banishing the police cars and garbage trucks. Thirty-Eighth and Chicago had been a hub of minority-owned businesses since the 1930s. But the future of these mom-and-pop shops was in doubt. Already reeling from the COVID-19 pandemic, the stores and restaurants had been cut off from their delivery drivers, suppliers, and customers. Uber and Lyft drivers couldn't get through, and a major bus route had been detoured around the intersection.

The residents of nearby houses and apartments were now stranded on an island created by the barriers. People felt like hostages in their own neighborhood, and some were *actually* hostages. Homeowners were being held up at gunpoint in front of their own garages and forced to pay a bribe so they could get their cars out of the alley and go to work. The surge in crime was astounding. In 2019, three people had been victims of nonfatal gunshot wounds in the area of Thirty-Eighth and Chicago. In 2020, that number rose to eighteen. Our ShotSpotter tracking system detected thirty-three rounds fired in 2019 and seven hundred the next year. That's a 2,000 percent increase in gunfire since the barricades went up.

Criminals seized the opportunity presented by the blockade; they could see the cops coming and knew we could only approach on foot. Responding to a shooting in the late summer of 2020, officers had to park their vehicles, walk in, and carry the wounded victim out to get medical care. The barriers delayed crime scene investigators' arrival at the site of another shooting. By the time they arrived, passersby had picked up many of the shell casings and contaminated the crime scene. As the weeks and months went on, we also received reports of drug dealing and sexual assaults near the memorial. The only people who seemed able to skirt the barriers were the carjackers who came from all over the city to drop off stolen vehicles in the cop-free zone.

The neighbors had said enough is enough. I spoke to Pastor Curtis Farrar, whose church was diagonally across the street from Cup Foods. Members of his congregation felt it wasn't safe for their families to attend Sunday service. Pastor Farrar understood that the community was in pain, and rightfully so. He was trying to do his part to foster healing, but outside the walls of his church was violence that he couldn't control. He told me he needed help to make sure that residents and visitors to the neighborhood were safe, and that safety was necessary for healing to begin.

I was acutely aware of the tragedy that happened at the intersection and its historical significance. And yet, the chief of police can't turn a blind eye to crime. I believe the extended shutdown of Thirty-Eighth and Chicago caused additional harm and was further traumatizing the people who lived nearby. As chief, I had an obligation to *all* of our residents. I believed we could maintain a permanent memorial to George Floyd *and* support the success of local businesses *and* prioritize the safety and health of the neighborhood.

However, the city's commitment to reopen the intersection was delayed, in part, by the ballot referendum that proposed eliminating the MPD. The city council had an agenda. They were not going to acknowledge that by isolating the area around Thirty-Eighth and Chicago, the city had unintentionally launched a case study in what happens when there are no police.

Eventually, however, there came a time when city leaders found it reasonable to hold two thoughts at once: We can honor George Floyd and open up the intersection. I got the green light from Mayor Frey to go ahead.

My first decision was to not use police or National Guard resources. I knew we couldn't send in people wearing the same uniform as the officer who caused the initial trauma at that location. If we were going to go in, we had to do it in a way that was respectful and had community support. I sat down with a notepad and began to plan the operation. It would require large numbers of public works employees, a convoy of loaders and trucks—and it had to be done quietly. Confidentiality would reduce the potential for a heated confrontation between city workers and groups that opposed reopening the square, but it wouldn't eliminate that risk. I would have to find a way to keep the public works crews safe without utilizing the police.

So, I approached the leaders of the Agape Movement, a respected nonprofit focused on criminal justice reform and preventing violence through boots-on-the-ground interaction in the community. Agape's reputation is earned because they're not fly-by-night. The leaders are from the community. I knew the people at Agape years before I became chief. We didn't always agree, but we had built a relationship over many years. When I asked them to take on security for this massive operation, they said yes. The Agape leadership saw that the blockade was causing harm to members of their community. It was their neighborhood, and they knew exactly what was going on there. Mr. Floyd had died by violence, the Agape leaders told me, and it wasn't right for his legacy to be *more* violence running amok in the neighborhood. They were not only concerned by the crime, but also by the sense of paralysis that had descended on what had been for decades an essential and vital neighborhood hub. Now it was as if the intersection of Thirty-Eighth and Chicago was a perpetual funeral, shadowed by clouds of grief that might never part. The people needed, and deserved, a sunny day.

I arranged a meeting in a community center conference room with public works supervisors and the Agape staff and volunteers who would be ensuring their safety. It wasn't lost on me that the public works supervisors were all white and the Agape members were all Black, and yet the two groups quickly built trust and understanding. Both groups knew that it wasn't right for anyone in the city to live with poor sanitation conditions and for children to see rats running around in the streets. It's not okay that neighbors can't get out in the winter because there are no snowplows to clear the way. Business owners shouldn't have to feel that they're sinking, and not just because of the pandemic, but because the city has shut them out. We were very clear that nothing would be done to alter Mr. Floyd's memorial. In fact, easing the traffic congestion, reopening access to public transportation, and addressing the crime and safety issues might bring in more people to say prayers and lay flowers. The Agape leaders saw that, and the public works supervisors saw that, too.

Every public works crew was assigned ten Agape members to accompany them. Agape's role was to run interference. If any members of the public tried to engage the city workers in a verbal or physical dispute, the Agape security teams would use their skills and training in de-escalation. I also put a quick reaction team of a dozen MPD officers on standby blocks away. That was the nuclear option, and we hoped we didn't have to use it.

We made headway during the night in removing the concrete barriers. When morning came, word of our operation got around and some people did come and shout at the work teams. I remember hearing one woman calling the city workers "white supremacists" and repeatedly yelling, "F— you!" But the work proceeded. The intersection was reopened to traffic. And the work crews didn't touch a single plant, flower, poster, gift, or photo that was part of the memorial. The iconic murals and the giant raised fists remain for all the visitors who come to honor the memory of George Floyd.

We have never blocked off streets for a year for any other homicide victim in the city. When there have been incidents of police misconduct, or even police killing of Black community members, there has been understandable anger, frustration, and sadness, and we've seen masses of people come together to speak out and protest for change. But I will also note that in the summer of 2021 when three young Black children under the age of nine were shot on the North Side, I did not see those massive rallies. We lost two precious, beautiful children, and a third is now disabled with a bullet lodged in his head. I didn't see the frustration boiling over then. I drove to North Memorial Hospital and held the hand of a heartbroken father at the bedside of his dying child. I didn't see thousands of people taking to the streets for his daughter.

I can only speculate why the community response and anger to commonplace violence is not proportional. One reason, I suspect, is that protesting police violence permits community members to hold another entity accountable—that is, the MPD. Yet, one of the reasons we need police is that community violence is occurring every day. How do we even begin to explain the senseless crimes that rob us of our young people before they even have a chance to start their lives? If we want answers, we are going to have to hold *ourselves* accountable. There was a time in our city when we wouldn't have needed $50—much less $180,000—to compel members of our community to share information about someone known or believed to have killed a child. In Minneapolis, eight out of ten victims of gun violence look like me, and nine out of ten perpetrators look like me. Ultimately, we in the Black community must come to the table and engage in the tough conversations necessary to bring about change.

We have stalwart leaders to guide us. After every one of those children was shot in 2021, Nekima Levy Armstrong, community elders, neighborhood activists, and faith leaders showed up. Their numbers were small, but their determination was limitless. They were not the only ones giving comfort and seeking justice for the children's families. There was also Lt. Richard Zimmerman, head of homicide, and his dedicated team of investigators. Together, we are the guardians along the watchtower. We don't always agree. We may find ourselves on opposite sides of a protest line. But we share an understanding that none of those lives—not George or Aniya or Trinity or LaDavionne—are disposable. Regardless of our differences, we believe we have an obligation and responsibility to our children and their future.

Immediately following the worst of the 2020 civil unrest in Minneapolis, I was invited to speak to a group of business owners whose shops and restaurants had suffered damage ranging from broken windows to looting to complete destruction. Many of those businesses were minority-owned or employed a large minority workforce. When I walked into a packed auditorium at the Colin Powell Leadership Academy just off Lake Street, the smoke was still rising from fires that had stretched for miles from east to west. There was not an empty seat in the audience, but there was plenty of room onstage. Although the mayor, city council members, and other city officials had also been invited, I was the only representative from the city of Minneapolis who showed up. I was tired and I probably looked it, with bloodshot eyes and the pallor of a man whose diet was mostly peanut M&M's.

I took the stage and started by giving updates. I kept expecting a backlash from the audience, given all that they had been through because of four of my former officers. I was ready to take it. But the audience members were simply appreciative that someone from the city had come to speak with them. They passed around a microphone. When one person spoke, everyone listened. Most of the business owners in the auditorium that day were members of our immigrant community. Many wanted to know how long the violence would go on. Some people were in tears. They were hurting, and they just wanted the truth. It was an intimate, vulnerable conversation and we all needed that.

Earlier that week I had been speaking to the owners and CEOs of large corporations to tell them that Minneapolis needed them now more than ever as pillars of the economic system our residents depend on. Some corporations can take a loss of millions of dollars. It was a stark contrast to the entrepreneurs at the Colin Powell Leadership Academy. In that auditorium, I had spoken to people who had spent their entire life savings to start a business that had just been looted, vandalized, or set on fire. Many had no insurance. Their livelihood was gone.

There's a cost to a crisis. In Minneapolis, much of that cost was borne by new arrivals who came to our city to chase what we call the American dream, to be good neighbors, and to provide a needed service.

As the microphone passed from hand to hand, I heard stories about the countries these business owners had fled to come here to start a new life. Some of these folks came from countries where corruption is part of the fabric of society, and they had experienced corruption in policing. They understood that conflict happens between police and the community. But nothing had prepared them for the video they had seen that showed a man dying in the street. They didn't understand it. They were horrified and devastated. "Why did the officer have to do that?" they said. "And then people burned our stores. We didn't do anything wrong. We didn't agree with what those officers did, and yet we also suffered."

I didn't have the answers they sought. "I can't tell you why individuals wearing the same uniform as me committed those horrible acts," I said. "But I can tell you they will be held accountable. You have my word on that. As long as I'm your chief, I'm not going to let you down. I will support you. I will be here for you. We're going to help this city and we're going to get back up. I'm so sorry for your losses."

Most people in the auditorium that day didn't have the same history as my family. They didn't know anyone who had been on Plymouth Avenue in 1967 or at the 4th Precinct in 2015. They didn't understand why the rage that took a foothold in the city destroyed a swath of the South Side and their livelihoods with it. They didn't understand why that rage was directed at them, people who were always good neighbors.

"But, Chief Rondo," they said, "we're not going anywhere. We're ready to rebuild. This is our city, and we're not leaving." There was a collective will to stay—not just to make a living, but to serve a community they had come to love. The same people who had been the victims of rage understood that such vengefulness was not truly who Minneapolitans are. They recalled the hundreds of neighbors and complete strangers who came with brooms and shovels to help them clear the rubble. That's who we are, they said. The worst thing they felt could happen was to compound one trauma with another. That secondary trauma would have been to say, we're all packing it in and that's it.

A middle-aged Latina woman took the microphone. She was emotional as she described opening her own panadería and not only serving delicious pastries and coffee, but also becoming a gathering place for neighbors, getting to know her customers, and employing local high school students for after-school jobs. As a business owner and a mother, she supported her children's schools. She was proud of her contribution to Minneapolis and the business she had created. But the panadería was gone. Burned to the ground. She turned to me, and then to the audience. "I can wallow in that grief and that would be understandable," she said. "Or, I can pick myself up and rebuild. And I choose that."

That's the story of Minneapolis. How on earth, after listening to her, could I feel anything but hopeful? I could only imagine the pain she must have felt, and yet I witnessed her resilience and faith. "As soon as we reopen," she said to me, "please have your officers stop by for a cup of coffee." If I live to be a hundred years old, it will not be enough time for me to thank her for her grace. She held true to her promise to me and her other neighbors. She didn't give up. To whoever lit the fire that consumed this woman's panadería, I hope you will see her in her new bakery on Lake Street today. And if you do, look inside your heart. What does your conscience say to you?

Regardless of our station in life, we all must decide how we are going to show up in the moment of crisis, and in the ongoing struggle. The people of Minneapolis are fighters. If we get knocked down, we get back up. At the end of the day, we take care of each other. Anybody that bets against Minneapolis is going to lose. We recognize our history, we see where we've fallen short, and we try to get better. But we are not a city that will allow one moment in history to define us. And so we continue to rise.

In the summer of 2020, we were living in a divided nation where political extremes had drawn us away from common ground. When face-to-face conversation is replaced with keyboard condemnation, when a smile and a greeting of hello is met with a condescending stare, when a disagreement is met with vitriol and backlash, that creates barriers and it depletes our bank of hope. I've seen it happen. That's why I refuse to give in to that way of thinking. We don't want to be so polarized that it takes a tragedy to bring us together. We shouldn't require a crisis to find our shared humanity. We should view each other as necessary every day. After Derek

Chauvin betrayed our badge and our city, I sought a new way to integrate humanity into every interaction that a police officer has with a civilian. Respect and caring must guide our actions from the moment we are sworn in as cadets. It all begins with the oath of office. Every policy, procedure, and training traces back to the values expressed in our oath. So I looked back in history—not just to the day of George Floyd's murder but also to the night I received a letter signed "KKK" and to the year I was born, when Plymouth Avenue burned. And I saw that the oath our officers had pledged for the past 155 years was not adequate. We didn't have an attachment to that promise, and too often we were breaking it.

When I reflected on where we needed to go, I understood that *all* are necessary to get us there. But only one point of view was represented in the oath, and that was the police department's. We needed a new promise focused on the needs and rights of the people we serve. They are our 430,000 bosses, and the police answer to them. Just days after George Floyd's murder, I reached out to Leslie Redmond, the president of the Minneapolis NAACP, and Steven Belton, president of the Minneapolis Urban League. I enlisted their partnership in writing a new oath for the MPD.

We began with a universal shared value: First, do no harm. This means that if I have to take an action that ultimately could create harm, that will be my last choice. The sanctity of life is paramount. It is critically important that officers go home to their families at the end of their shift, and that civilians should go home to their families at the end of their interaction with police. There is nothing in the oath that says this pledge applies only to the *good* citizens. Even if a person is a suspect, or is belligerent, or has been caught committing a crime, officers still have an obligation to uphold the sanctity of their life. We must safeguard everyone in our custody, with no exceptions.

The new oath continues: "I will shield and protect my community from those who would seek to cause harm." It says *my* community, not *the* community. It doesn't matter whether an officer comes from Hibbing, Minnesota, or New York City—once they take the oath, Minneapolis is their community. And the members of that community come first. The new oath states that an officer shall intervene in protest both verbally and physically if they witness anyone violating someone's rights, even if that person is a police officer. This pledge acknowledges the imbalance that exists between civilians and police. Only the police have the right to detain someone or use deadly force if justified. So police must hold each other accountable. Our oath is a solemn promise to be there for our communities and to do right by the people. We do not have to be perfect, but we must do right by them. If an officer breaks this promise, they will have to live with that. But I don't have to live with them in this organization anymore.

The final line of the new oath is the most revolutionary: "I recognize those I serve are members of the human family worthy of dignity and respect, and my term in office shall be guided by my love of service to the community and the grace of humanity." The most important word that we inserted into this new oath of office is "love." Every day around the country and in my city, courageous men and women who wear this uniform rush toward the sound of gunfire—all to protect the lives of strangers. How do they do that without hesitating? It's love. It's because they have a love for their fellow human beings and it doesn't matter if the person they protect is Republican or Democrat, white or Black, or who they pray to. The police are there to help. That's why I got into this profession, and that's why I believe policing is an honorable calling.

Policing is not a job that you should ever take for the paycheck. Officers spend a great part of their careers being called into people's lives at their darkest moments. Police are witnesses to the greatness that human beings possess and to the evil that exists among us. We are called to be a light, a beacon of hope, a champion of justice, and a fair arbiter of disputes. Some members of our communities may not even want us there. But good police are needed. I believe that the vast majority of police officers will do the right thing even when nobody's watching. But, like the great experiment that is American democracy, American policing must continue to evolve and grow—and that is my dream.

I was first sworn in as an MPD cadet in 1989. It was one of the proudest moments of my life. Three decades later, I raised my right hand again—this time, as chief—and uttered a new oath to define a new era in the MPD. I believe this new oath will have an impact on our city, and on the department, long after the memory of my time as chief has faded. The previous oath lasted for 155 years. I believe the new one is worthy of standing just as long.

George Floyd's murder was arguably the most significant killing of a civilian by a police officer in modern history. I knew that what occurred at Thirty-Eighth and Chicago on May 25, 2020, was forever going to change my life and the life of my city. Near dawn the next day, during the brief pause before the nation woke up to see Darnella Frazier's video, I took a moment to think long-term. As chaotic as the coming weeks would inevitably be, I knew I was going to get through this, and so would Minneapolis. I was also wondering: What would my life look like after? What would the department look like?

Leaders can't pick and choose the crises they face. This one had happened on my watch, during a pandemic, with an oppositional union president and city council members who caused me to wonder repeatedly where all the grown-ups had gone. It seemed that the only thing normal about my five-year term as chief was the unprecedented. I was in a position to guide the city through the crisis of 2020—but history has shown that the one who leads the revolution is not the one who should lead the change. I had a role in that place and time, but I knew all along there would come a day when I would have to move on.

By December of 2021, one-third of the officers employed by the MPD in 2020 had left the department. The community had ousted Bob Kroll from law enforcement altogether. The voters had defeated a ballot measure to eliminate the MPD, and the same election had shaken up the city council. A lot had changed, and I felt that I had to be a part of those changes, too. The community was starting to go from pain to healing to recovery after the conviction of Derek Chauvin. If I stayed another term, however, I would still be defined by my actions in 2020. It was time to look to the future, and that meant it was time for me to go. I invited Mayor Frey to dinner to tell him I would not seek another term as chief. He wanted me to stay. I told him I felt that he needed new police leadership. The next part of the journey was not meant for me.

I felt at ease with my decision, as well as my timing, while the mayor and I planned a press conference to announce that I would be retiring from the MPD. But before I stepped up to the podium to share the news publicly, I made two phone calls. The first was to Don Damond, who had shown me years before what grace looks like. Don is a reason I will forever believe in hope. When an MPD officer shot his fiancée, Justine Damond, Don lost the most important human being in his life. And what did he do? He wanted to help build something bright from such a dark tragedy. In time, Don met with me and said, "Justine would want your men and women to be better, to be their best selves. She truly believed in the positive transformation of mindfulness training and, Rondo, we're going to do that for your officers." Even though he was grieving, he was not going to let Justine's death be the last chapter. He rolled up his sleeves and found a way to change the MPD for the better, and for the benefit of the citizens of Minneapolis. At first, his grace and kindness took me aback. But the more I learned from Don about his beloved Justine, the more I understood that he was carrying on her legacy of hope and healing.

When Don picked up the phone, I said, "I want you to hear from me first that shortly I'm going to announce my retirement from the MPD." My appointment as chief was inextricably linked to Justine's tragic death and she has never been far from my thoughts. I said, "I hope, Don, that I served in a way that you and she would have approved of. I did my best, even though I was far from perfect." I thanked Don for the kindness that he showed me personally, the grace that he showed the department, and for helping us to embrace health and wellness. He thanked me and said, "Rondo, I hope you are well and I look forward to hearing what your next journey will be."

My next call was to Ben Crump, the attorney for George Floyd's family. I left Mr. Crump a voicemail requesting that he please convey to Mr. Floyd's family that I'd be announcing my retirement. I wanted to extend again my deep apologies for the loss of their loved one and I wanted them to know I tried my best to get justice for George Floyd. I hope I did all right by them.

Of course, I had already shared the news of my retirement with my family. I thanked my son and daughter for being there with me every step of the way during my career, even though they never signed up for it. I told them, not for the first time, that if there's any good that I've achieved in my life it's because of them. I apologized to them as well for the precious time that I missed with them. I hoped they would forgive me. My children said they were proud of me, they loved me, and they were very happy that now I would not be taking on so much. They said, "Dad, it's time. You put so much into your job. The past few years you have been under a constant barrage. Now you can spend time with us, without your cell phone going off." And they were right. It has been a great joy in my retirement to celebrate the birth of my son's first child, and to walk my daughter down the aisle at her wedding.

I had also called my parents to tell them I was retiring. My mother would have been furious if she saw it on the news first! She was emotional, as mothers can be, and told me she was proud. My dad was more stoic. "Good job," he said. A month later at a community celebration of my retirement held at Shiloh Temple, my parents were seated in positions of honor onstage. My mother stood up and spoke extemporaneously. She spoke about the fear and anxiety she felt for more than thirty years being the mother of a police officer. Every morning, she would text me to wish me a good day. Every night, she would text me good night. Sometimes she didn't hear back from me for weeks, but she understood. Her son was a busy man with an important job, a dangerous job. My mother looked around at all the people seated in the pews and made a sweeping gesture. She said, "I worried about my son every day. But I didn't realize that, all along, there was a whole community looking out for him."

I had gone through a long career and received promotions and departmental awards. But nothing made my heart feel more right than when I came to the end of the road and the people who had so closely watched my journey told me I had done well. Bishop Howell also spoke that night. He said, "We saw you, we appreciate your family for lending you to us, and you did a good job." That was more valuable than any paycheck I ever received. I knew that I was rich in life. My community didn't always agree with me, but there was never one day when I felt they didn't support me.

I've been blessed to be a son of Minneapolis. I was raised to recognize the importance of hope, and that's what drove me every day of my career. Hope is saying that despite all the pain and trauma that our communities are experiencing, there is still a better tomorrow.

17

A Better Place for You

Dear Gianna,

I know we have never met and yet over the past few years you have been a motivating factor for the decisions I've made and the actions I've taken.

Gianna, I never met your father, but after he was taken from you I made two promises to him that I never got to tell him, so I would like to share those with you in this letter. That first promise was to make sure I spoke up on his behalf to let others know that his life was not disposable and that those responsible for his death would be held accountable.

Dearest Gianna, the second promise I made to your father was that I would find the words one day to let you know that I'm so painfully sorry that your father is no longer here, that he can no longer watch you celebrate your birthdays, see you advance to the next grade in school, hear you laugh loudly after he does something funny, or that he can't be there to put his arms around you and give you a big hug to reassure you that everything's going to be all right when you feel scared or unsure.

Gianna, on that tragic and sad day, even though I wasn't there, I heard your father. He was never alone. Gianna, as you continue to grow and live your life, you may have questions as to why someone would harm your father, especially someone who took a promise to protect and serve their community. Gianna, I may never know the answer to that question. However, I want you to know when your father spoke out that he was hurting and needed help, . . . I heard him. When your father cried out "Mama. I'm through," . . . I heard him. When the people on the street corner demanded that the officer stop hurting your father, . . . I heard them. When people around the world proclaimed enough is enough, . . . I heard them. When the judge told me to raise my right hand and swear to tell the truth, . . . I heard him. When twelve people who didn't know your father but honored their civic duty to listen to all the facts and evidence—and came back with a decision of guilty against those responsible for your father's death, . . . I heard them. Gianna, when you said "Daddy changed the world," . . . I heard you. Now, at this time, Gianna, as you read my letter, I hope you hear me when I tell you I'm deeply sorry. Your father should still be here with you to delight in your achievements and see you become the incredibly intelligent, compassionate, strong, and resilient person you will be.

Gianna, if you should ever read this letter, please know that in many ways our lives will be connected by your father, so in that sense there is a bond we will have with each other always. Gianna, I have chosen to let that space that connects me to your father be about *hope*. I believe your father would want that for me and I have a strong feeling he would want that for you, too.

Gianna, lastly, I want you to know, as a father myself, how proud and inspired I am by you. I've watched you from afar knowing your father is no longer here physically, yet you carry his spirit and smile with you. As young as you are, I've watched how you share your story of how proud of him you were—and you do so with an infectious smile that, as a father, makes me beam with joy. Gianna, you remain an inspiration to me and so many others. Gianna, I believe adults everywhere have an obligation to *all* our children to *never* remain silent when we witness harm against humanity. To remain silent means we are complicit, so we *must* act. Gianna, I promise you that I will do all I can during the time I'm given to make this world a better place for you.

With Love and a Promise,
Chief Rondo

Afterword

FEBRUARY 3, 2025

In this new chapter of my life, I am able to continue a life of service inspired by my community and my experiences in the MPD. Today I serve on the board of Urban League Twin Cities, an organization that has contributed positively to the African American community in Minneapolis for nearly a hundred years, dating further back than even the time of Edith and Arthur Lee. I also serve on the board of Fentanyl Free Communities, a local organization fighting the opioid epidemic in Minneapolis. I got involved because of an encounter I will never forget. Years ago, I was driving in my squad car on a sweltering hot day and answered a call about an overdose. The paramedics were on their way, but I arrived first. I got out of my squad and saw a man on the ground. He was dying. When I knelt down next to him, his breath was almost gone. That's when I noticed a note pinned to his shirt. It said: "The NARCAN is in my pocket." I had arrived too late to administer the lifesaving antidote. I saw then how the drug makes you dance with death. And the overwhelming odds are, you'll never finish that dance. So, when I had the chance, in my retirement, I knew I had to do something to help.

One of the many positions I held during my time in the MPD was an assignment as an undercover public housing enforcement officer in the early 1990s, when gangs were taking over the apartments of elderly and vulnerable residents to sell crack cocaine. I saw the victimization of a population that tends to be invisible in our city, and I understand what safe and dignified housing means to people. My experience working in public housing helped me to be a better chief. So I ran for a seat on the Minneapolis Board of Public Housing, where I can continue to serve a community that I have never forgotten.

I'm no longer a police chief but there is still a role for me to play to help the profession evolve in America and around the world. I continue to do what I can to make sure that we reach that dream of policing systems that are fair, just, and worthy of the public's trust. I've been contacted by governments and law enforcement agencies around the world that are facing challenges or trying to implement cultural change and build new leadership. Today, when I am on a video call with the head of the national police in Liberia, the photo of Henry G. Thompson can still be seen in the background, hanging above my desk in my home office. His photo continues to remind me that history is not an anchor. We must study it, embrace it, and carry its lessons forward into the future.

Notes

CHAPTER 1

Ancestry.com. Information on William J. Meehan on "Find a Grave," accessed October 2024. https://www.findagrave.com/memorial/207258520/william-j.-meehan.

Boogren, Jill. "GFS: Sowing Seeds of Solidarity," *Longfellow Nokomis Messenger,* September 2, 2024. https://www.longfellownokomismessenger.com/stories/gfs-sowing-seeds-of-solidarity,6667.

Davis, W. Harry, and Lori Sturdevant. *Overcoming: The Autobiography of W. Harry Davis.* Afton Historical Society Press, 2002.

Donofrio, Greg. "A Right to Establish a Home." Goldstein Museum of Design, University of Minnesota, August, 2014. https://humantoll35w.org/owningup/wp-content/uploads/2018/11/RightToEstablishAHome_Final-greg-donofrio.pdf.

Editorial Board, "Reaction to the Plymouth Ave. Uprising," *Minneapolis Tribune,* July 25, 1967.

Hall, Chatwood. *The Crisis,* October 1931.

Juergens, Ann. "Lena Olive Smith: A Minnesota Civil Rights Pioneer," *William Mitchell Law Review* 397, 2001. https://open.mitchellhamline.edu/facsch/61/.

Marks, Susan. "Civil Unrest on Plymouth Avenue, Minneapolis, 1967," Minnesota Historical Society MNopedia, December 21, 2015. https://www.mnopedia.org/event/civil-unrest-plymouth-avenue-minneapolis-1967.

Meitrodt, Jeffrey. "For Riot-Damaged Twin Cities Businesses, Rebuilding Begins With Donations, Pressure on Government," *Minneapolis Star Tribune,* June 6, 2020. https://www.startribune.com/for-riot-damaged-twin-cities-businesses-rebuilding-begins-with-donations-pressure-on-government/571075592.

Poferl, Greg. "The Arthur & Edith Lee Family Story," *East Side Freedom Library Blog,* August 24, 2020. https://eastsidefreedomlibrary.org/the-arthur-edith-lee-family-story/.

Shabazz, Rashad. "Minneapolis' 'Long, Hot Summer' of '67—and Parallels to Today's Protests Over Police Brutality," *Minneapolis Spokesman,* June 6, 2020.

https://spokesman-recorder.com/2020/06/06/minneapolis-long-hot
-summer-of-67-and-parallels-to-todays-protests-over-police-brutality/.

Sluss, Jackie. "Lena Olive Smith: Civil Rights in the 1930s," *Hennepin History Magazine*, Winter, 1995, Vol. 54, No. 1. https://hennepinhistory.org/lena -olive-smith/.

Welter, Ben. "Angry White Mob Surrounds Minneapolis Home," *Minneapolis Tribune,* July 16, 1931.

Yuen, Laura. "When Flames of Racial Strife Engulfed a Minneapolis Street," Minnesota Public Radio News, July 19, 2017. https://www.mprnews.org /story/2017/07/19/minneapolis-plymouth-avenue-riots-anniversary.

CHAPTER 2

Burnside, Tina. "Southside African American Community, Minneapolis," Minnesota Historical Society MNopedia, February 1, 2017. https://www .mnopedia.org/place/southside-african-american-community-minneapolis #:~:text=The%20Southside%20was%20a%20stable,the%201930s%20to%20 the%201970s.

CHAPTER 4

African American Registry. "'The Way' Community Center (Minneapolis) Opens." Accessed May, 2024. https://aaregistry.org/story/the-way -community-center-minneapolis-opens/.

Anti-Defamation League. Bigots on Bikes: The Growing Link Between White Supremacists and Biker Gangs. September 2011. https://www.adl.org/sites /default/files/documents/assets/pdf/combating-hate/ADL_CR_Bigots_on _Bikes_online.pdf.

Hankin-Redmon, Eric. "Near North African American Community, Minneapolis," Minnesota Historical Society MNopedia, January 15, 2020. https://www.mnopedia.org/place/near-north-african-american-community -minneapolis.

KARE-11 News. "Girl in Critical Condition After Being Shot in Head in Minneapolis Saturday Night," Minneapolis, May 16, 2021. https://www .kare11.com/article/news/local/child-shot-while-playing-saturday-night-in -minneapolis/89-79679efb-d84f-4acb-9a69-7e0b2c57a2c1.

KARE-11 News. "Family Says 9-Year-Old Shot in Head While Playing on Trampoline Has Died," Minneapolis, May 27, 2021. https://www.kare11.com

/article/news/crime/family-says-9-year-old-shot-in-head-while-playing-on
-trampoline-has-died/89-5b877c50-8cbc-4925-8676-82d7c7f77a51.

Maddox, Camille Venee. "The Way Opportunities Unlimited, Inc.: A Movement
for Black Equality in Minneapolis, MN 1966-1970." BA Thesis, Emory
University, 2013.

Michaels, Samantha. "Minneapolis Police Union President Allegedly Wore a
'White Power Patch' and Made Racist Remarks," *Mother Jones*, May 30, 2020.
https://www.motherjones.com/criminal-justice/2020/05/minneapolis
-police-union-president-kroll-george-floyd-racism/.

Minnesota Compass. Community data accessed May, 2024. https://www
.mncompass.org/profiles/city/minneapolis.

CHAPTER 5

Baker, Myriam L., Jane Nady Sigmon, and M. Elaine Nugent. "Truancy
Reduction: Keeping Students in School," *Juvenile Justice Bulletin*, US
Department of Justice, September 2001.

Tiesman, Hope M., PhD; Katherine L. Elkins, MPH; Melissa Brown, DrPH;
Suzanne Marsh, MPA; and Leslie M. Carson, MPH, MSW. "Suicides Among
First Responders: A Call to Action." *Centers for Disease Control and Prevention
NIOSH Science Blog*, April 6, 2021. https://blogs.cdc.gov/niosh-science-blog
/2021/04/06/suicides-first-responders/.

Walsh, Paul. "Ex-Minneapolis Police Officer Convicted of Sexually Abusing
Teen in Hotels, Squad Car." *Minneapolis Star Tribune*, October 17, 2018.
https://www.startribune.com/ex-minneapolis-police-officer-convicted-of
-sexually-abusing-teen-in-hotels-squad-car/497847901/.

CHAPTER 6

City of Minneapolis 2022 Gun Violence Review. August 2, 2022.

Kian, Ava. "The Ripple Effects of Gun Violence in Minnesota," *MinnPost,* April
5, 2024. https://www.minnpost.com/race-health-equity/2024/04/the-ripple
-effects-of-gun-violence-in-minnesota/#:~:text=%E2%80%9CThe%20
most%20likely%20victim%20of,Criminal%20Justice%20at%20Hamline%20
University.

Minnesota Department of Employment and Economic Development. "Report
on Minnesota Economic Disparities by Race and Origin," February, 2024.
https://mn.gov/deed/data/.

MPR News Staff. "Minnesota Health Care Systems Label Gun Violence a Public Health Crisis," *Minnesota Public Radio News*, June 8, 2022. https://www.mprnews.org/story/2022/06/08/minnesota-health-care-systems-label-gun-violence-a-public-health-crisis.

CHAPTER 7

Jimenez, Omar, and Eric Levenson. "Former Minneapolis Police Officer Mohamed Noor Released From Custody After Over 3 Years Behind Bars," CNN.com, June 27, 2022. https://www.cnn.com/2022/06/27/us/mohamed-noor-justine-ruszczyk-release/index.html.

Minnesota Department of Corrections public information database. https://coms.doc.state.mn.us/PublicViewer/Home/Index.

Smith, Mitch. "A 911 Call, an Unarmed Woman and a Single Shot: The Mystery of a Police Shooting," *New York Times*, April 13, 2019. https://www.nytimes.com/2019/04/13/us/mohamed-noor-trial-minneapolis.html.

Smith, Mitch. "Minneapolis Police Officer Receives Shorter Sentence in Fatal Shooting," *New York Times*, October 21, 2021. https://www.nytimes.com/2021/10/21/us/mohamed-noor-minneapolis-sentenced.html.

CHAPTER 8

Bergin, Daniel. "100 Years After the Duluth Lynching, Another Face Is Added to the 'Mob' of Systemic Racism," Twin Cities Public Television website, June 11, 2020. https://www.tptoriginals.org/100-years-after-the-duluth-lynching-another-face-is-added-to-the-mob-of-systemic-racism/.

Julin, Chris, and Stephanie Hemphill. "A Mob Lynches Three Black Men," *Minnesota Public Radio*, June 2001. https://news.minnesota.publicradio.org/projects/2001/06/lynching/page1.shtml.

Minnesota Department of Human Rights. *Investigation into the City of Minneapolis and the Minneapolis Police Department*, April 27, 2022. https://mn.gov/mdhr/assets/Investigation%20into%20the%20City%20of%20Minneapolis%20and%20the%20Minneapolis%20Police%20Department_tcm1061-526417.pdf.

Minnesota Historical Society. "Duluth Lynchings: Resources Relating to the Tragic Events of June 15, 1920." Accessed September 3, 2024. https://www.mnhs.org/duluthlynchings/lynchings.

NOTES

Photograph of Henry G. Thompson and his family. Minneapolis Police Museum, November 5, 2020. https://mplspolicemuseum.org/our-earliest -badge-is-worn-again-today/.

Video: Remarks from Dr. Josie Johnson at the swearing-in ceremony of Medaria Arradondo as Minneapolis Chief of Police. https://youtu.be /zmjoY8-5BjQ.

CHAPTER 9

Furber, Matt, and Mitch Smith. "Minneapolis Officers in Jamar Clark Shooting Will Not Face Charges," *New York Times*, March 30, 2016. https://www .nytimes.com/2016/03/31/us/jamar-clark-shooting-minneapolis.html.

Smith, Mitch. "Police and Protesters Clash in Minneapolis Over Fatal Shooting of Black Man," *New York Times,* November 19, 2015. https://www.nytimes .com/2015/11/20/us/minneapolis-protest-police-jamar-clark.html.

US Department of Justice Office of Public Affairs. "Federal Officials Decline Prosecution in the Death of Jamar Clark," June 1, 2016. https://www.justice .gov/opa/pr/federal-officials-decline-prosecution-death-jamar-clark.

CHAPTER 12

Alcorn, Chauncey. "One Year After George Floyd's Murder, Minneapolis' Businesses Are Still Reeling," CNN Business, May 25, 2021. https://www .cnn.com/2021/05/25/business/minneapolis-businesses-after-floyd-protests /index.html.

Allen, Karma. "Man Who Helped Ignite George Floyd Riots Identified as White Supremacist," ABC News, July 29, 2020. https://abcnews.go.com/US /man-helped-ignite-george-floyd-riots-identified-white/story?id=72051536.

Bierschbach, Briana. "Gov. Tim Walz Laments 'Abject Failure' of Riot Response," *Minneapolis Star Tribune,* May 29, 2020. https://www.startribune .com/gov-tim-walz-laments-abject-failure-of-riot-response/570864092.

Bradner, Eric. "Minnesota Gov. Tim Walz Tries To Calm Minneapolis After Days of Chaos Following George Floyd Killing," CNN.com, May 30, 2020. https://www.cnn.com/2020/05/30/politics/tim-walz-minnesota-george -floyd-killing/index.html.

Buchanan, Larry, and Quoctrung Bui. "Black Lives Matter May Be the Largest Movement in US History," *New York Times,* July 3, 2020. https://www .nytimes.com/interactive/2020/07/03/us/george-floyd-protests-crowd-size .html.

NOTES

Burch, Audra D.S., Weiyi Cai, Gabriel Gianordoli, Morrigan McCarthy, and Jugal K. Patel. "How Black Lives Matter Reached Every Corner of America," *New York Times,* June 13, 2020. https://www.nytimes.com/interactive /2020/06/13/us/george-floyd-protests-cities-photos.html.

CBS News. "'When the Looting Starts, the Shooting Starts': Trump Tweet Flagged by Twitter for 'Glorifying Violence,'" May 29, 2020. https://www .cbsnews.com/news/trump-minneapolis-protesters-thugs-flagged-twitter/.

Elizabeth, De. "Billie Eilish, Beyoncé, Ariana Grande and More Celebrities Respond to George Floyd's Death," *Teen Vogue*, May 31, 2020. https://www .teenvogue.com/story/celebrities-respond-george-floyd-death#:~: text=Celebrities%20including%20Beyonc%C3%A9%2C%20Taylor%20 Swift,their%20fans%20to%20get%20involved.

Fox 9 News, Minneapolis. "Future Affordable Housing Lost Due to Flames During Minneapolis Riot," Fox 9 News, May 28,2020. https://www.fox9 .com/news/future-affordable-housing-lost-due-to-flames-during -minneapolis-riot.

Gerlicher, Scott. *Written Testimony of Commander Scott Gerlicher, Minneapolis Police Department,* Testimony before the Minnesota State Senate, August, 2020. https://townsquare.media/site/669/files/2020/09/Written-Testimony -Scott-Gerlicher.pdf.

McNamara, Audrey. "Minnesota Governor Fully Mobilizes State's National Guard," CBS News, May 30, 2020. https://www.cbsnews.com/news/tim -walz-minnesota-governor-fully-mobilizes-national-guard-first-time-in -history-george-floyd-death-protests/.

Palmer, Annie. "Read the Email Tim Cook Sent to Apple Employees About George Floyd," CNBC, May 31, 2020. https://www.cnbc.com/2020/05/31 /apple-ceo-tim-cook-email-to-employees-about-george-floyd.html.

Smith, Savannah, Jiachuan Wu, and Joe Murphy. "Map: George Floyd Protests Around the World," NBC News, June 9, 2020. https://www.nbcnews.com /news/world/map-george-floyd-protests-countries-worldwide-n1228391.

Starr, Barbara, Sarah Westwood, Lauren Fox, and Sunlen Serfaty. "White House Wanted 10k Active Duty Troops To Quell Protesters," CNN.com, June 7, 2020. https://www.cnn.com/2020/06/06/politics/white-house-10k-troops -protesters/index.html.

Twitter account of Donald J. Trump, May 28, 2020. https://x.com/White House45/status/1266342941649506304?lang=en.

United Nations. "Eliminating Racism: Time for Change," *The Yearbook of the United Nations,* accessed September 4, 2024. https://www.un.org/en /yearbook/eliminating-racism-time-change.

CHAPTER 13

ACLU Minnesota. "Nekima Levy Armstrong et al. v. City of Minneapolis et al., United States District Court, District of Minnesota," p. 8, March 11, 2021. https://www.aclu-mn.org/en/cases/nekima-levy-armstrong-et-al-v-city -minneapolis-et-al.

ACLU Minnesota. "Statement on Settlement With Former MPD Union Head Bob Kroll," April 4, 2023. https://www.aclu-mn.org/en/press-releases/aclu -mn-statement-settlement-former-mpd-union-head-bob-kroll.

Anti-Defamation League. *Bigots on Bikes: The Growing Link Between White Supremacists and Biker Gangs.* September 2011. https://www.adl.org/sites /default/files/ADL_CR_Bigots_on_Bikes_online.pdf.

Bjorhus, Jennifer. "Fired Minnesota Officers Have a Proven Career Saver: Arbitration," *Minneapolis Star Tribune,* June 21, 2020. https://www.startribune .com/minnesota-cops-fired-then-rehired/571392702.

City of Minneapolis Officer Complaint History Dashboard, accessed September 12, 2024. https://www.minneapolismn.gov/government /government-data/datasource/officer-complaint-history-dashboard/.

Civil Rights Litigation Clearinghouse. "Case: Levy Armstrong v. City of Minneapolis." https://clearinghouse.net/case/43094/.

Collins, Jon. "Half of Fired Minnesota Police Officers Get Their Jobs Back Through Arbitration." Minnesota Public Radio News, July 9, 2020. https:// www.mprnews.org/story/2020/07/09/half-of-fired-minnesota-police -officers-get-their-jobs-back-through-arbitration.

DeRusha, Jason. "Full Interview: Lt. Bob Kroll, MPD Union Officials Condemn Derek Chauvin's Actions, Say City Is Scapegoating the Union," WCCO News, June 23, 2020. https://www.cbsnews.com/minnesota/news/interview -mpd-unions-lt-bob-kroll-condemns-derek-chauvins-actions-says-city-is -trying-to-scapegoat-the-union/.

Gockowski, Anthony. "Retired Police Union President Bob Kroll Reacts to New Settlement," Alpha News, April 6, 2023. https://alphanews.org/retired -police-union-president-bob-kroll-reacts-to-new-settlement/.

Hartman, Chad. "Former Mayor R.T. Rybak Says Police Federation President Is a 'Cancer,'" WCCO News Radio, May 29, 2020. https://www.audacy.com /wccoradio/articles/feature-article/former-minneapolis-mayor-police -federation-president-cancer.

Jany, Libor. "Controversy Follows Minneapolis Police Union President," *Minneapolis Star Tribune,* December 11, 2015. https://www.startribune.com /controversy-follows-minneapolis-police-union-president/361517061.

Jany, Libor. "Firing of Minneapolis Officer Who Struck Handcuffed Man Reduced to 2-Week Suspension," *Minneapolis Star Tribune*, December 6, 2019. https://www.startribune.com/firing-of-minneapolis-officer-who-struck-handcuffed-man-reduced-to-2-week-suspension/565749592?refresh=true.

Jany, Libor. "Minneapolis Officer Fired for 2016 Beating of Handcuffed Man; Partner Also Faces Termination," *Minneapolis Star Tribune*, February 18, 2019. https://www.startribune.com/minneapolis-police-officer-fired-for-2016-beating-of-handcuffed-native-man-partner-also-faces-termination/506012022.

Jany, Libor. "Minneapolis Police Officer Fired for Decorating Racist Fourth Precinct Christmas Tree Gets Job Back," *Minneapolis Star Tribune*, August 25, 2020. https://www.startribune.com/minneapolis-police-officer-fired-for-decorating-racist-fourth-precinct-christmas-tree-gets-job-back/572098402.

Jany, Libor. "Newly Released Surveillance Video Shows Punching Incident That Led to Minneapolis Officers' Firing, Rehiring," *Minneapolis Star Tribune*, December 13, 2019. https://www.startribune.com/newly-released-surveillance-video-shows-punching-incident-that-led-to-minneapolis-officers-firing-re/566189181.

KARE-11 News. "Settlement Bars Former MPD Union Head From Police Work in 3 Metro Counties," April 4, 2023. https://www.kare11.com/article/news/local/courts-news/settlement-bars-bob-kroll-from-police-work-in-3-metro-counties/89-e275e4cb-6b31-4df9-98ae-05e09f118597.

Levinson, Reade, and Michael Berens. "Special Report: How Union, Supreme Court Shield Minneapolis Cops," Reuters, June 4, 2020. https://www.reuters.com/article/world/special-report-how-union-supreme-court-shield-minneapolis-cops-idUSKBN23B2LQ/.

Mahaffey v. Kroll, Casetext.com (Thomson Reuters). https://casetext.com/case/mahaffy-v-kroll/.

Mahaffey v. Kroll, United States District Court, District of Minnesota, August 20, 2008. https://d3n8a8pro7vhmx.cloudfront.net/cuapb/pages/270/attachments/original/1532851583/Mahaffy_v_Kroll_et_al_Art_a_Whirl_Incident_20080822.pdf?1532851583.

Michaels, Samantha. "Minneapolis Police Union President Allegedly Wore a 'White Power Patch' and Made Racist Remarks," *Mother Jones*, May 30, 2020. https://www.motherjones.com/criminal-justice/2020/05/minneapolis-police-union-president-kroll-george-floyd-racism/.

Moini, Nina. "Mpls. Mayor Vows To Fire Cop for Racist 4th Precinct Decorations," Minnesota Public Radio News, November 30, 2018. https://

www.mprnews.org/story/2018/11/30/minneapolis-police-racist-christmas
-decoration.

Rosario, Ruben. "Minneapolis Police Union Head: Unapologetically Tough,
Aggressive," *Pioneer Press*, June 10, 2016. https://www.twincities.com/2016
/06/10/minneapolis-police-union-president-bob-kroll/.

Scheiber, Noam, Farah Stockman, and J. David Goodman. "How Police Unions
Became Such Powerful Opponents to Reform Efforts," *New York Times*, June 6,
2020. https://www.nytimes.com/2020/06/06/us/police-unions-minneapolis
-kroll.html?unlocked_article_code=1.E04.BFED.VBR-skKyvTPV&smid
=url-share.

Sepic, Matt. "Police Chief Plans April Hire of North Mpls. Precinct Inspector,"
Minnesota Public Radio News, February 22, 2019. https://www.mprnews
.org/story/2019/02/21/arradondo-minneapolis-fourth-precinct-inspector
-yet-to-hire.

Simon, Alexandra. "Former Minneapolis Chief Shares Letter From Police
Union President on George Floyd, Calls for His Badge," KARE-11 News,
June 2, 2020. https://www.kare11.com/article/news/local/george-floyd
/minneapolis-police-union-president-officers-in-george-floyd-case
-terminated-without-due-process/89-fa7fb13a-d167-472e-bf3c-e2d625
9f8f6d.

Thiede, Dana. "Group of Minneapolis Police Officers Writes Open Letter
Condemning Chauvin, Embracing Change," KARE-11 News, June 11, 2020.
https://www.kare11.com/article/news/local/george-floyd/group-of
-minneapolis-police-officers-write-open-letter-condemning-chauvin
-embracing-change/89-1c837d8e-29a2-419a-baf3-61fc55ba590c.

CHAPTER 14

CNN.com video. "What the Minneapolis Police Union Leader Said at a 2019
Trump Rally." https://www.cnn.com/videos/politics/2020/06/01
/minneapolis-police-union-president-praise-trump-campaign-rally.cnn.

Collins, Jon. "Justice Department Offers Assistance to Minneapolis Police,"
Minnesota Public Radio News, October 20, 2020. https://www.mprnews
.org/story/2020/10/20/justice-dept-offers-assistance-to-minneapolis-police.

Furst, Randy. "Minneapolis Cops Working Lynx Game Walk Out Over Player
Comments, Warm-Up Jerseys," *Minneapolis Star Tribune*, July 12, 2016. https://
www.startribune.com/minneapolis-cops-working-lynx-game-walk-out
-over-player-comments-warm-up-jerseys/386373171.

Jany, Libor. "Minneapolis City Council Committee Nixes Applying for Federal Grant for More Cops," *Minneapolis Star Tribune*, March 4, 2020. https://www.startribune.com/minneapolis-city-council-committee-nixes-applying-for-federal-grant-for-more-cops/568501422.

Levy Armstrong, Nekima. "Black Voters Need Better Policing, Not Progressive Posturing," *Minneapolis Star Tribune*, November 10, 2021. https://www.startribune.com/black-voters-need-better-policing-not-progressive-posturing/600115233?refresh=true.

Minneapolis Police Department Crime Data Analysis, October 2021.

Minnesota Public Radio News. "Department of Justice Announces New Initiative," Facebook Live video, October 20, 2020. https://www.facebook.com/MPRnews/videos/3346266965411159.

Minnesota Twins. "Jim Pohlad, Executive Chair," accessed September 12, 20204. https://www.mlb.com/twins/team/front-office/jim-pohlad.

Minnesota Twins. "Twins Announce Plans for 2020 Home Opener," July 23, 2020. https://www.mlb.com/twins/press-release/press-release-twins-plans-for-2020-home-opener.

Schwartz, Ian. "Minneapolis City Council President on Dismantling Police: Wanting to Call the Police 'Comes from a Place of Privilege,'" *Real Clear Politics*, June 8, 2020. https://www.realclearpolitics.com/video/2020/06/08/minneapolis_city_council_president_on_dismantling_police_wanting_to_call_the_police_comes_from_a_place_of_privilege.html.

Yglesias, Matthew. "The Case for Hiring More Police Officers," *Vox*, February 13, 2019. https://www.vox.com/policy-and-politics/2019/2/13/18193661/hire-police-officers-crime-criminal-justice-reform-booker-harris.

CHAPTER 15

Allen, Jonathan. "Minneapolis Police Chief Testifies Chauvin Violated Policy in George Floyd Arrest," Reuters, April 5, 2021. https://www.reuters.com/world/us/minneapolis-police-chief-expected-testify-against-chauvin-murder-trial-over-2021-04-05/.

Associated Press. "Ex-Minneapolis Police Officer Sentenced to 57 Months in the Killing of a 911 Caller," NPR, October 21, 2021. https://www.npr.org/2021/10/21/1047986308/mohammad-noor-sentenced-minneapolis-police-911-australian-caller.

Griffith, Janelle. "The 'Blue Wall of Silence' Is Crumbling in the Derek Chauvin Trial. Why This Case Could Be a Tipping Point," NBC News, April 7, 2021.

https://www.nbcnews.com/news/us-news/how-derek-chauvin-s-trial
-bringing-down-blue-wall-n1263383.

Jimenez, Omar, and Eric Levenson. "Former Minneapolis Police Officer
Mohamed Noor Released From Custody After Over 3 Years Behind Bars,"
CNN, June 27, 2022. https://www.cnn.com/2022/06/27/us/mohamed
-noor-justine-ruszczyk-release/index.html.

Laughland, Oliver. "Derek Chauvin Trial: Police Chief To Testify Against Former
Officer in 'Remarkable Move,'" *The Guardian*, April 2, 2021. https://www
.theguardian.com/us-news/2021/apr/02/george-floyd-derek-chauvin-trial
-police-chief-testimony.

Lopez, German. "Police Officers Are Prosecuted for Murder in Less Than 2
Percent of Fatal Shootings," *Vox,* April 2, 2021. https://www.vox.com
/21497089/derek-chauvin-george-floyd-trial-police-prosecutions-black
-lives-matter.

Mapping Police Violence, accessed September 1, 2024. https://mappingpolice
violence.us/.

Office of Public Affairs, US Department of Justice. "Former Minneapolis Police
Officer Derek Chauvin Pleads Guilty in Federal Court to Depriving George
Floyd and a Minor Victim of Their Constitutional Rights," December 15,
2021. https://www.justice.gov/opa/pr/former-minneapolis-police-officer
-derek-chauvin-pleads-guilty-federal-court-depriving-george.

Office of Public Affairs, US Department of Justice. "Former Minneapolis Police
Officers Tou Thao and J. Alexander Kueng Sentenced to Prison for Depriving
George Floyd of His Constitutional Rights," July 27, 2022. https://www
.justice.gov/opa/pr/former-minneapolis-police-officers-tou-thao-and
-j-alexander-kueng-sentenced-prison-depriving.

Walsh, Paul, Abby Simons, and Hannah Sayle. "A Day-by-Day Recap of the
Derek Chauvin Murder Trial," *Minneapolis Star Tribune*, April 20, 2021.

Walsh, Paul, Abby Simons, and Hannah Sayle. "Who Were the Witnesses in the
Derek Chauvin Trial?" *Minneapolis Star Tribune*, April 15, 2021. https://www
.startribune.com/who-are-the-witnesses-in-the-derek-chauvin-trial-for-the
-killing-of-george-floyd-in-minneapolis/600042794.

Wurzer, Cathy, Ellen Finn, and Melissa Townsend. "Judge Peter Cahill Reflects
on High-Profile Trials, Allowing Cameras in Courtroom," Minnesota Public
Radio News, October 11, 2022. https://www.mprnews.org/episode/2022
/10/11/judge-peter-cahill-reflects-on-highprofile-trials-allowing-cameras
-in-courtroom.

Acknowledgments

If there has been any good in my life, it has been my son, Medaria Vangmoua, and my daughter, Nyasia Kashia. You have been on this journey with Dad from the beginning, as children watching me put on my "costume" every day for work and as young teens understanding that, because of my job's unpredictability, I would miss some of your athletic events or choir concerts at school. Now, as young adults seeing me try to make up for that lost time, you both have given me such grace and care—which is your way of showing that my debt has been settled. I love you more than life itself.

I am a representation of my parents. To my dear mother and father, thank you for giving me life and love. You showed me through your examples that we treat others the way we want to be treated, and that hate should never find refuge in our hearts or home.

To my siblings, the Arradondo clan, I love you all and I am blessed to be your brother.

Sarah, Adonis, Jaida, Lyric, and Tianna—sending you all my love.

To my ancestors, thank you for the strength of your dreams. Your aspirations—envisioned before I was born and passed down to me from a different time and place—made it possible for me to lead.

To my elders, the kings and queens of my Minneapolis community, thank you for your wisdom, guidance, mentorship, and the struggles you endured on my behalf.

To the Floyd family and Mr. Don Damond, may you always be surrounded in peace and comfort. Your loss will forever be a part of me, and I am forever indebted to you for the grace you have shown me. God bless you.

Courtney Ross, you are a light that sees the good in us. You reassure us that we do not have to be defined by our past. I admire your strength and selflessness and thank you for your friendship.

Darnella Frazier, your courage and compassion forced all those who watched your video to heed the warning that silence is complicity. Thank you.

Nekima Levy Armstrong, my unconventional ally, who by a singular action trusted me and shaped the future. Thank you for giving me the benefit of the doubt that I would do the right thing. This story could not be told without you.

To dear Dr. Josie Johnson, our Minnesota matriarch of civil rights, thank you for leading by example and leading the way.

To our very own freedom fighter, Elder Spike Moss.

Mayor Jacob Frey, you gave me your unwavering support and you also believed that we as a city would get through those exceedingly difficult days. Thank you.

Minnesota Attorney General Keith Ellison, The Hon. Jerry Blackwell, and attorney Steve Schleicher, your respectful and exceptionally professional pursuit of truth and justice is to be commended.

Rainer Drolshagen, I woke you up in the early morning hours needing your assistance and you delivered. Thank you for your service and for taking my call.

Mariah, thank you for your love and support.

Corey Lyell, my brother and best friend, much love and respect.

Jermar Arradondo, thank you for our special cousinship and your fierce support of me since childhood. You brought the team together and I look forward to what the next journey holds.

To the amazing Jennifer Amie, we're two South Side Minneapolis kids who came into each other's lives for a reason. You are now a part of my family, and you were the only one who could have authored this book. I cannot wait to read your next works. Jo and Alden, you both are so talented and wonderful.

The guru Lionel Coleman, you came into my life and saw something in me and this story that needed to be told so that future generations would benefit from it. You are a great director and storyteller. I appreciate you and Michelle so much.

Michael McConnell, you are the best manager, and I can't thank you and Zero Gravity Management enough for your friendship and the immense protection and care for this book.

Ian Kleinert and the great Paradigm team, you knocked on doors so that this book could happen. Thank you, Ian.

Keith Wallman and the talented Diversion Books crew, thank you for embracing and investing in our story. Keith, you are awesome. Thank you.

Christopher Noviello, a phenomenal filmmaker and funny guy. I enjoyed our afternoon brainstorming sessions. Thank you.

John Klassen and Andy Muller, the dynamic duo of attorneys. Thank you for your superb legal representation and friendship over the years.

To my incredible MPD leadership team, Mike, Henry (rest in paradise, my dear friend), Eric, Kathy, Art, John, Cyndi, Nina, Tasha, and Danielle, thank you for your exemplary dedication and service you delivered every day to the people of Minneapolis.

To MPD Chief Robert K. Olson (ret.), thank you for exposing me to leadership early on in my career. I learned a great deal from you and I'm forever grateful.

DC Greg Hestness and DC Bill Jones, I appreciate your mentorship and support.

ACKNOWLEDGMENTS

Former chiefs Scott Thomsen and Michael Davis, I cannot thank you both enough for leaning in during those difficult days offering your sage counsel and support.

Erica MacDonald, when our city needed help and was being denied critical resources, you showed up and asked what you could do to help. Your assistance made a difference. Thank you.

Bill Bratton, I have appreciated your incredible public safety insight and support over the years. Thank you.

Giovanni Veliz, mi amigo and respected leader. I continue to learn a great deal from you. Thank you.

Dr. Oneica Benn and her students in Brooklyn, New York. Your students are the heroes in our community. Thank you for preparing our next generation of kings and queens.

Scott and Diane Thompson, thank you for your friendship and care.

Thank you, Alan Hilburg, Jill Sanborn, Michael Paul, Chief Todd Axtell, Leon Carroll Jr., Leslie Redmond, Steven Belton, Yolanda Wilks, Laura Stearns, Doug Baker, Jim Pohlad, Minneapolis Roosevelt High School, International Entrepreneurs' Organization, Inspector General Gregory Coleman of the Liberian National Police, Russell Ambrose, Latoya Turk, Patty Hamm, Linda Menar, Mike Carey, Melvin Ferguson, Glenn Burt, Glen Henry, Mong Lee, Ker Yang, Candice Mama, Rose Kingston, Agape Movement, and Unity Community Mediation Team.

To the men and women who wear a badge and serve their communities here in the United States and around the world in a procedurally just way, with a love of service, yours is indeed a noble calling and an honorable profession. Continue to remember that we are all a part of the human family, and all are necessary.

My best,
Rondo

ACKNOWLEDGMENTS

Rondo, you gave us hope when we needed it most. You led our hometown through chaos with kindness, respect, and reason. You took a stand and refused to look the other way. You showed us what true leadership looks like. Thank you for trusting me to help you tell your story.

To my husband, Jo Amie, for believing in me and supporting me every step of the way. Thank you for always being by my side. As the first reader of this manuscript from its earliest drafts, your insights, queries, and counsel are woven into these pages.

Alden, you are my favorite person. I'm thrilled to see your talents as an artist and writer bloom. I may be the first in our family to publish a book, but it won't be long before you are next.

To Jermar Arradondo, my lifelong friend, thank you for being the catalyst that made this book possible.

Thank you to Michael McConnell of Zero Gravity Management and to Ian Kleinert and the team at Paradigm Talent Agency for your guidance and for advocating that this story be told.

Keith Wallman, you are the editor of my dreams! You inspired trust from the first time we met. You share your knowledge and expertise with a generous spirit. All your contributions have made this book the best it can be. What an incredible experience it has been to work with you.

Sarah, Kristin, Megan, Emily, Jeffrey, Jennifer, Michael, Trina, and Mary, your support and encouragement means the world to me.

Lionel Coleman, you have shown me by example what is possible when you put your mind to it. Your talent is limitless. You are the best creative partner I could hope for.

Christopher Noviello, thank you for being a champion of this story.

ACKNOWLEDGMENTS

To Nekima Levy Armstrong, for standing on the watchtower. You are an inspiration.

To Minneapolis, my hometown.

My best,
Jennifer

About the Authors

MEDARIA "RONDO" ARRADONDO, a son of Minneapolis, was appointed the city's first Black chief of police in 2017. He has gained international recognition for his role in leading through the George Floyd crisis, securing justice, and implementing police reforms while enhancing transparency. Rondo retired in 2022 after thirty-two years of service in the Minneapolis Police Department. Today he is president and CEO of Optimus Sui Consulting, LLC. Rondo works with global leaders in government and law enforcement to advance procedural justice and advises corporate clients on crisis management and leadership. He remains active in Minneapolis as a commissioner of public housing and an executive board member of Fentanyl Free Communities.

JENNIFER AMIE is a born-and-raised South Minneapolis native. A writer with deep roots as both a magazine journalist and a staff writer for educational institutions, she specializes in the worlds of art, culture, nature, science, and people who are catalysts of change. She also writes and produces documentary films and will be an executive producer for

ABOUT THE AUTHORS

the upcoming documentary film *Rondo*. After graduating from Minneapolis South High School, she received a BA from Reed College and an MA in journalism from the University of Minnesota. She resides in Portland, Oregon.